EBURY PRESS

THE AUTOBIOGRAPHY OF GOD

Lenaa Kumar is an award-winning actor, clinical psychologist, scriptwriter and entrepreneur renowned for her impact on Indian cinema over a career spanning more than twenty-five years. Having pursued acting from the age of sixteen, she has worked in over 175 films in five languages, delivering blockbusters and critically acclaimed performances in English, Hindi, Tamil, Telugu and Malayalam films. She has won numerous awards, including Filmfare, SIIMA, IIFA, International Film Festival of South Asia Toronto, Kerala State Film and Kerala Film Critics Association awards. An active advocate for mental health, emotional well-being and self-awareness, she is a transformational speaker on a mission to empower with self-realization through infotainment. Her TEDx talk has been viewed more than 9,50,000 times.

Email: theautobiographyofgod@gmail.com
YouTube: theautobiographyofgod, Lenaasmagazine
Instagram: lenaasmagazine, theautobiographyofgod
Facebook: realizewithlena
Websites: theautobiographyofgod.com and lenaalife.com

T0267834

THE AUTOBIOGRAPHY OF GOD

Self-Realization in 5 Practical Steps

LENAA KUMAR

EBURY
PRESS

An imprint of Penguin Random House

EBURY PRESS

USA | Canada | UK | Ireland | Australia
New Zealand | India | South Africa | China | Singapore

Ebury Press is part of the Penguin Random House group of companies
whose addresses can be found at global.penguinrandomhouse.com

Published by Penguin Random House India Pvt. Ltd
4th Floor, Capital Tower 1, MG Road,
Gurugram 122 002, Haryana, India

This edition published in Ebury Press by Penguin Random House India 2024

10 9 8 7 6 5 4 3 2 1

ISBN 9780143466840

Typeset in Adobe Caslon Pro by Manipal Technologies Limited, Manipal

www.penguin.co.in

This book is dedicated to You, the reader,
who is also I.

Yes!

The title is a joke.

It gets really funny when you wake up to the first-person experience of it and funnier still when you try to explain it.

Contents

CONSCIOUSNESS
WHO AM I?

BLISS
WHERE, WHEN AND WHY AM I?

Gratitude

The Autobiography of God would not have been possible without you . . .

My dear parents, Mohankumar Thathampilly and Tina Mohankumar, thank you for bringing me into this world and instilling in me the values and beliefs that have shaped my journey. Grateful to the ancestors who were self-content and allowed me the freedom to pursue Self-Realization.

To all who have been my Gurus, thank you for showing me the way and guiding me towards infinite wisdom.

Prasanth, my mirror, my All.

Words cannot convey my gratitude to my editor, Premanka Goswami, and to Madhu, for making me a Penguin author. A very special thank you to Suchitra Mohanlal, for connecting me to Premanka. I am honoured to be working with the best at Penguin Random House: Vineet Gill, Vijesh Kumar, Aakriti Khurana, Ahana Singh and the whole team who have made this book what it looks like.

Tasha, thank you for your unconditional love.

Abhi, thank you for being everything you've been to me.

Mohan B., my esoteric psychotherapist, thank you for listening to me blabber for over a decade until I found the actual words to express my thoughts.

Richard, eternally grateful to you for being more than a friend in need and for the spiritual horizons you opened up for me.

Mohan, Fred and Harish, Remya, Anushree, Ashwin, Raje, Aslam, Louisa, Netto, Manikandan, Saxon, Vipin, Vrinda, Ramlu, Radhika, Suresh Peters, Jayakrishnan N., Ike, Annie, Mithran, Ratheesh Vega, Lijo, thank you for being part of my adventures!

Geetika Saigal, thank you for being my guide throughout this book's journey.

Rajeev Nair, thank you for being the first reader of this book. Your feedback truly gave me the courage to continue on this path. A very special thank you for polishing my words and guiding me.

Jinson Abraham, thank you for being the amazing photographer you are and making me look so good on the cover.

Thank you, Helen, for converting my handwritten manuscript to digital text.

A very special namaste to you, Anamay, for showing me that a pure mind that is ready responds with spontaneous enlightenment on reading and listening to these words.

Annliya, Ananthu and team Shadow, your sincere involvement with social media, marketing and so much more is a true blessing.

Hari Bhagirath, thank you for the insightful strategies.

Immensely grateful to Sri Mohanlal for introducing me to the Vigyan Bhairav Tantra and being such an enigmatic inspiration.

Eternally grateful to Sri Murali Gopy for directing the mind and heart towards wisdom instead of superstition.

Always grateful to Sri Joju George for guiding me towards healing through self-belief and Ayurveda.

Ever grateful to Dr Vipin and Sri Murali of AYV.

Sincere love and gratitude to Sri Adil Hussain and Dilip for the experience of meditation.

Vishen Lakhiani and Mindvalley, thank you for introducing me to a world of mentors, including Robin Sharma, Anodea Judith, Marisa Peer, Michael Bernard Beckwith, Ken Wilber, Jeffrey Allen, Neale Donald Walsch and yourselves.

Eternally grateful to Chinmaya International Foundation and Br Ved Chaitanya.

Grateful to everyone who has been part of my life, everyone, everywhere, all at once. Thank you!

Disclaimer

The information in this book is not intended to diagnose, treat or serve as medical advice. Please consult your health practitioner regarding any prescribed medication. Do not stop taking any medication based on the information in this book. This book does not promote the use/abuse of psychotropic substances.

Introduction

'There is nothing more enjoyable than doing the impossible.'
—Walt Disney

What would you say if I told you there is a single comprehensive answer that could remove all the miseries from your life?

The answer is: 'Enlightenment'.

Do you think you could be an Enlightened/Self-Realized Being?

If your answer is no, you have plenty of company.

Humanity's greatest self-limiting belief is that self-realization or Enlightenment is impossible for the common person.

Believing that Enlightenment is possible and must be everyone's top priority in this lifetime is the only requirement for it to happen.

The only way out of stress, confusion, anxiety, mania and depression is to know oneself. All else is temporary relief and half-hearted survival.

Enlightenment is everyone's birthright.

If this sounds like a 'get-rich-quick' scheme, it is because this book offers you exactly that. But the riches are not material. You become rich in wisdom.

Wisdom is a self-realized experience. I can take you through that by guiding you as you answer five basic questions.

Let me tell you through this book how I know this can be done.

It's crazy how it started. I did not have recourse to the five simple questions when I was confused and suffering through the proverbial 'dark night of the soul'. All that clouded my mind was one big question: 'What the hell is going on here?'

However, when I found the answer, I could not prove it, defend it or even articulate it in words.

After eighteen years of struggling to share this wisdom, I finally came upon a system of 'Five Basic Questions' that will lead you to personally discover that 'One Answer'.

So, if you would like to know the 'One Answer', here are the 'Five Basic Questions':

What, who, where, when and why am I?

If you can answer those five questions, to your own satisfaction, this book is not for you.

If you are not satisfied with your own answers, let me show how you can change your entire life.

This book is not about:
Philosophy
Mystical thinking
Lists of affirmations
Religious dogma

This book is for:
The rational
The logical
The practical
The seekers
The non-conformists
The leaders
The pioneers
The rebels and free spirits

The Autobiography of God contains practical tools for the new age of humanity.

Right now, we are at an unprecedented time in history when our earth's consciousness is shifting. If you want to shift with it and if you want to emerge in the new age, namely, the **Age of Self-Realization** that is beyond the **Age of Information,** then you need to know what lies ahead and, most importantly, what lies within.

Anyone who has mastered the Self has shared their findings in the simplest words such as 'Know Thyself' or 'Be a light unto yourself'. They observed so because it is the easiest thing to do. Really.

It is easier to know oneself than know anything else. It is easier to know the whole than know it through all its parts.

As the **Age of Enlightenment** dawns, the whole earth, including the earthlings, is moving towards a spontaneous waking up. This process can be confusing if we are not prepared for it.

This book is a humble attempt to prepare the reader for the process of waking up or Self-Realization. It does not have to be an esoteric experience. It is the very nature of everything and the foundation upon which individual life is built. The first step in demystifying Self-Realization is to answer the logical and rational questions of the mind. The magic happens on its own, once the rational and logical aspects are satisfied.

From the questions of 'what, who, where, when and why am I?' to a comprehensive subjective experience of 'what, who, where, when and why I am', every question answered contributes to a spontaneous 'Aha!' moment.

Let's begin destroying humanity's biggest self-limiting belief and living out our full potential.

Do you say, 'My Body?'

Do you say, 'My Mind?'

Who is claiming ownership of the body and mind? Who is saying Mine?

The immediate answer is usually: 'I am.' So, the next logical question is 'Who am I?' Change the question to get the answer.

In trying to express the inexpressible, words, syntax and grammar need to be twisted and bent to point to the ineffable. The only hope is that these peripheral aspects, like waves on a sea, do not distract the reader. Instead, I wish you the clarity that allows the mind to go deep where there are no waves and experience Consciousness Bliss.

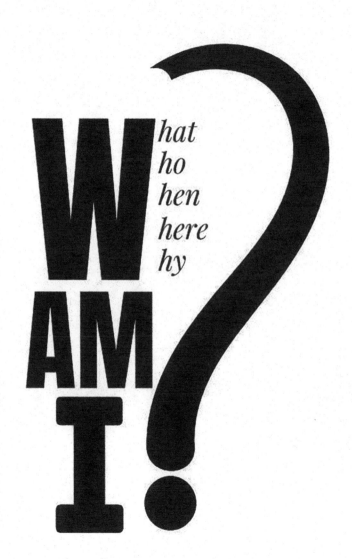

EXISTENCE

WHAT AM I?

1

Lenaa in Wonderland

'The world is illusory, only Brahman is real. Brahman is the world.'

—Adi Shankaracharya

That misty morning, on 3 September 2004, in the pine forests of Kodaikanal, a hill station in south India, a group of excited twenty-something-year-olds stumbled upon a patch of shiny white mushrooms growing out of bison dung.

I was twenty-three years old, in the first year of being married to my childhood sweetheart, and full of questions. As I sat under a pine tree, chomping on a mushroom and wondering what Alice in Wonderland must have experienced, I found myself moving into a meditative trance.

In that moment of Self-Realization, which I will only comprehend much later, the most basic of my doubts gathered prominence: 'What is God? What is going on here?'

A while later, I found my body lying on the soft earth covered in layers of pine leaves. The warm morning sun was caressing my cheek in that cold, crisp, clean air. I tried to think, but somehow, I couldn't.

This inability to think made me feel like my heart was in a deep embrace and blossoming into a realm I had never realized before.

An unknown calm, yet feeling very familiar, filled me. That feeling of 'myself', which had remained unchanged through all my twenty-three years on earth, became so strong that it made me sit up straight. I opened my eyes.

The orange moss on the pine tree trunks was fluorescent. I hadn't noticed it until that moment. The mist was little drops and not a continuous sheet. My body was breathing in and out along with all the plants, trees and earth. My heart was full and my mind empty. Closing my eyes and sitting still, I became aware that I was not my body, my mind or my energy. I was that sense of self that I now know as Awareness. The silent message was loud and clear: 'awareness that is aware of itself is God'.

Time ceased to exist, and a calm ecstasy filled me completely. I knew God! And I knew God as me. It all seemed so simple and ordinary.

Noticing that our friends were walking deeper into the forest, I got up from the spot I had been rooted to for what seemed an eternity. Running up to my husband to share my experience, the impossibility of it hit me. Words wouldn't form and my tongue felt like lead.

We walked on in silence. Reaching a cliff at the top of the hill, I stood at the edge holding on to a small tree, and looking at the steep drop and the valley below.

My friends' voices seemed to come from light years away, though they were just a few feet from me. They were all frantically telling me to step away from the edge. I looked back and smiled, feeling no fear or urgency as a huge passing cloud engulfed us.

Nothing but cold white existed.

2
Megalomania?

'I am like an idiot. My mind is so empty I am different from ordinary people. I drink from the infinite.'
                                    —*Lao Tzu*, **Tao Te Ching**

Having reached for the secret too soon, unprepared for what to do with the answer, silence was my only refuge.

On 5 September 2004, back in Bangalore city, my husband opened the floodgates with the question. 'What happened to you?'

Words flowed out of my mouth in lumps—ugly and insufficient.

I heard myself say, 'Lenaa is over. A whole lifetime flashed across my mind in reverse order and in slow motion . . . Life is not what we thought it was, I can hear others' thoughts.' I was rambling.

Trying hard to sound sensible and solve the confusion, I blurted out, 'The point is, I am God and so are you and everything else.'

I don't recall the expression on his face or what happened over the next few days. There were just a lot of questions, concerns, friends in and out of the house, friends living with us, and, finally, my parents and sister turning up.

Apparently, I had not eaten or slept for seven days while speaking continuously, trying to explain the satori. I went from weighing 70 kilograms to 54 kilograms, from familial mundane conversations to verbal diarrhoea, and from a clinical psychologist to a psychiatric patient in just seven days.

Being labelled manic depressive and needing psychiatric medication lifelong was not something God was willing to put up with. All God wanted was to Be.

Thank you for joining me on this journey of how I turned every breakdown into a breakthrough and how you can too.

For, as Kurt Cobain said, 'All in all is all we are.'

3

Tell Yourself the Truth

'I've been through some terrible experiences in my life and some of them actually happened.'

—Mark Twain

Telling the truth, the whole truth, and nothing but the truth definitely needs God's help. Lying to oneself is the best way to keep the ego alive. The way out is to know everything. And to know everything all you need to know is **you.**

I have heard Robin Sharma tell this story . . .

One day a little boy was pestering his father to play with him while the father was really busy with important work. The father spotted a picture of the globe in a newspaper near him and tore it into small bits and handed it to his son and said, 'Put these pieces in place to form the complete globe.' Smiling at his ingenuity that would keep the little boy busy for quite a while, the man got busy again.

In less than a few minutes the boy was back with the completed picture of the globe!

His father couldn't believe it. The son gave him a big toothy grin as he explained, 'On the other side of the globe there was a picture of a man. Once I got the man, the world was all right!'

The Ego = Ignorance

The ego: *A false sense of Self, created by the mind to protect itself from the unknown.*

The truth: The one and only undeniable truth that holds true subjectively, as a sense of rightness, can be mutually agreed upon by two individuals as well as appear as a fact when looked at in the third person. It can be described in one word: PERSPECTIVE.

This is the ultimate wisdom an enlightened being arrives at. Life, which is conscious energy, condenses into multi-dimensional manifestations, including physical forms, to have a unique experience and expression, aka perspective of itself.

A perspective experienced and expressed in the Hear–Now is what is meant by 'Being'. We are not beings (human or otherwise) having a perspective. We are perspectives of Life. Other than one's own perspective, nothing else can be known. Just as one can never know the perspective of another one of Life's forms. It is truly a miracle that we can seem to understand a perspective different from our own, let alone synergize or include it within us. The difference in an individual and a Self-Realized Being is that the individual has a point of view of things, while the Self-Realized Being has an all-inclusive perspective of everything and nothing together as the one whole that is the Self. The Self-Realized One is overjoyed to experience all the different expressions of perspective and immediately includes it into the whole picture.

If you truly desire to evolve spiritually, learn to pay attention to others' point of view and imbibe as much of it as may help you evolve, while allowing the parts that don't resonate with you to just remain in the whole, undisturbed by you. As you evolve to wholeness, you become all-inclusive. All opposites get neutralized within your wholeness of perspective, and you do not experience or express separateness. Only allowance and resonance remain.

4

What I Am
Is What I
Identify With

'The worst part about having a mental illness is
people expect you to behave as if you don't.'
—***Arthur Fleck** in* Joker

For those of us who often forget that 'normal' only means 'average', pursuing normalcy becomes a goal gifted by well-intentioned and poorly informed family, friends and society.

10 September 2004

Every nerve from the tip of my toes to the top of my head was aching, pulling and pushing as a cocktail of psychiatric drugs tried to bring the extraordinary back to 'normal'. In all that dazed confusion I still kept thinking,

'What went wrong?'

I felt deep within me the clarity of my experience but the medicines had begun to plant doubts in my mind. My mind had started to crawl back and it was supposed to be kept in that state of mundaneness through medication for the rest of my life at the expense of my kidneys, liver, heart and, of course, my brain.

As I struggled to make sense of my realization of the self and the situation I found myself in, the nosedive into depression began. Between September and November 2004, I glimpsed the freedom of liberation, and then plunged into the dark night of the soul.

To understand these states better, I will put them to you as five levels of identification.

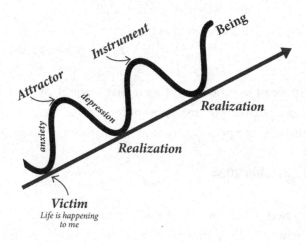

Figure 1: Four Levels of Identification

1. The victim: Life is happening to me
2. The attracter: Life is happening for me
3. The instrument: Life is happening through me
4. The creator: Life is me
5. The Bliss: Life is all there is (No Me)

Clearly, the peak experience or satori of 3 September was a brief visit to the level-four consciousness of being, oneness, ultimate or absolute oneness with all things, aka Self-Realization. The subsequent state was a plunge to stage-one consciousness or victim consciousness where the predominant theme is blame, shame and depression.

I do not advocate or justify the use of psychedelics, natural or man-made, for this exact reason and many more. However, the world over, more and more studies are supporting the therapeutic and spiritual value of psychedelic plant medicine such as psilocybin and ayahuasca, among others.

The consciousness and mind-expanding capabilities of psychedelics are best experienced when used as medicine or during a spiritual ceremony—meaning, when approached with reverence, care, caution and responsibility, and not for fun, recreation or escaping reality and oneself.

The effects are intense and if not done with a conscious purpose and guidance from a guru, doctor or shaman, it could have disastrous consequences.

I am one of those lucky few who got out of the victim state of this experience, having studied psychology, having been a meditator for a few years prior to meditating on the magic mushrooms in the forest, and having a clear question or direction in which the experience could go, namely, 'What is ultimate reality?'

However, it took me fourteen years of being on psychiatric medication while also working to prove my self-worth, being self-sufficient and learning all the alternative methods of dealing with stress, anxiety and depression, to break free and live without medication.

5

The Victim
(I Am the Body)

Life Is Happening to Me

'If you think you can or you think you can't, either way you are right.'

—Henry Ford

The most common question of someone who feels like a victim is, 'Why me?!'

This just means that consciousness identifies with the body and is deluded by the belief 'I am the body'.

Changing the typical victim question of 'Why is this happening to me?' to 'What is happening to me?' is the first baby step out of depression. Follow it up with more empowering questions such as, 'What is this situation trying to teach me?', 'What else is possible?', 'What can I do to get out of this situation?', 'What would the ideal situation be?' and so on.

Anxiety is commonly defined as an overwhelming feeling of worry, nervousness or unease about something with an uncertain outcome.

Depression is defined as a mental condition characterized by feelings of severe despondency and dejection, typically also with feelings of inadequacy and guilt, accompanied by a lack of energy and disturbance of appetite and sleep.

While studying psychology at the graduate and postgraduate levels, I had wondered what the subjective experience of these problems would be like and whether they were just symptoms of deeper issues.

Now from personal experience, I see **anxiety as the mind's reaction to a huge change in consciousness. The experience of leaving one's comfort zone. It is more like a warning sign of moving into the great unknown or being at the gates of change. If understood from a point of evolving consciousness, then it is really a moment of celebration!**

When pure consciousness begins to dawn in the heart, if the mind is not prepared, the physical sensation is similar to death, a heart attack or suffocation. This is called a 'panic attack'.

Anxiety often precedes a huge life-changing moment of realization and depression usually follows it.

Depression, in this sense, is the letting go of the previous self-image, and the time the mind takes to adjust to its new realization of having left the old comfort zone.

The thing to keep in mind is that change is messy, frightening and takes work. Despite the state you are in, you need strong motivation to get started. For most people, as it was with me in the beginning, the greatest motivator is 'I will show them'—the need to prove and earn one's self-worth.

Mood disorders are usually classified as cyclical in nature. However, their subjective experience is that they are either upward or downward spirals, not cycles.

Let's take the upward spiral as an example:

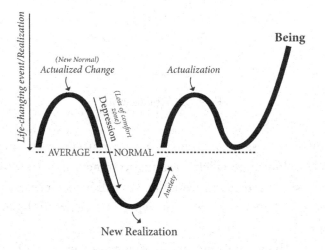

Figure 2: Upward Spiral

One will clearly realize that the upward movement towards change or realization is when anxiety hits. After the realization, the downward movement is the sinking in of the realization and the actual implementation of the change that causes a sudden shift from one's comfort zone—which is termed depression. It is after one such whole cycle that a person's personality changes and the level of consciousness

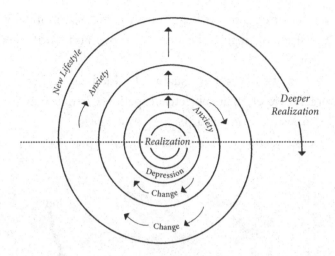

Figure 3: Actualization

evolves. For someone who is into evolution, cycle after cycle follow quite quickly, leading to something that looks like a spiral staircase. I would like to call it the 'stairway to heaven'. Once one stops identifying as a victim and gains control of one's life the spiral seems easier.

Try drawing a wave and marking your journey of ups and downs on it. You will begin to see the pattern.

6

The Attractor
(I Am the Mind)

Life Is Happening for Me

'If you really want something, the whole universe conspires with you to achieve it.'

—*Paulo Coelho,*
The Alchemist

I had always believed in magic and miracles. In a way, I'm always a child. However, my belief in the ability to manifest the life of my dreams became stronger in 2004. In psychiatric language, this is called **magical thinking** and was one of the many symptoms on my psychiatrist's list, which had other interesting symptoms such as **novelty seeking**.

The one motivator I used in November 2004 was, 'I will prove them wrong.' 'Them' being my psychiatrist and immediate family. But to prove them wrong I had to prove myself right! I had no idea where to start. The only words of solace in my heart were: 'Nothing can destroy that which is true. The truth will prevail.'

The heaviness of past success of being a good student and receiving a scholarship from my father's company since the fourth grade, being a Kerala state rank holder for my bachelor's degree in psychology from Calicut University and having had my own earnings as a film actor since the age of sixteen weighed heavily on me in November 2004, when I was broke and labelled psychologically ill.

Sitting at the dining table in my parents' apartment in Thrissur, Kerala, tears streaming down so profusely that they could have made grooves in my shrunken face, I was thinking of ways to end my life.

The second wave of thoughts began to draw on the first. They said, 'It's just depression. Suicidal ideation is just a symptom. Lenaa, what do you want now to get out of this?' The therapist in me had woken up and has never left since. I followed this reassuring voice, my higher self!

The tears were a warm river on my face as I knelt before the statue of Saint Anthony at the church while the Sunday mass progressed. I hadn't been to a church in a long while. I kept saying, 'Show me the way, show me the way, show me the way. I will not get up from here till you show me the way.'

The mass was over, and the congregation left. My parents were standing helplessly outside wondering what to do with me. 'Show me the way, show me the way,' I went on. My mother came up to me and motioned for me to come outside. I refused. She said, 'I had a phone call from Asianet television network's PRO, Mr Praveen. They wanted to know if you would play the lead in their new TV series.'

Looking up at the statue of Saint Anthony I broke into a wide conspiratorial grin. This timely miracle healed the depression but now anxiety took over. I kept thinking, 'Will I be able to act?'; 'They are casting me based on my looks from a year before I quit films for marriage'; 'They will reject me at the sight of me now,' and on and on it went.

The writer of the series, its producer and Mr Praveen from Asianet came to my parents' house to meet me. I hadn't slept for days and could barely make eye contact. I struggled to smile over the insecurity that was crushing me like a huge boulder on my head. Then, the writer, Mr Joicy, announced, 'I was sceptical about casting you, as the heroine of my show must look beat down, depressed and weak. Now I'm sure you would be perfect for the role.'

The universe conspiring with me began to feel like the oneness of me again. The ability to cry all day without glycerin too turned out to be a blessing while filming for the series *Omanathingal Pakshi*, which went on to become the most popular TV show of its time and got me back on my feet and back into cinema. Television also fetched me my first Kerala State Award for Best Actress.

My inner turmoil was numbed thrice a day with medication. The heartbreaking feeling was due to the life sentence that the pills came with. Life went on.

In 2006, the film and the book *The Secret*, by Rhonda Byrne, took the world by storm. I remember reading the book on a flight and trying out the steps in the book immediately. It said, '**Ask**. **Believe**. **Receive**.' So, I asked that my bag be the third on the conveyor belt upon arrival. I believed, as I always did, and the green leather bag was the third when the belt started moving.

I couldn't control my joy and smiled to myself knowing that all is well. Magical thinking was gaining popularity or rather becoming normal!

By 2008, I had forgotten my existential angst (anxiety) and was mastering the state of **attractor consciousness**. From the need to prove myself to others, I had become interested in proving what more was possible to me.

I wrote a wish list for the year, in January 2008. On the list to be manifested were,

1. Money
2. An apartment of my own
3. Travel
4. To act with Mohanlal, the leading actor from Kerala, India

By December 2008, I had made the exact sum of money I had envisaged, bought an apartment and travelled to the places I had earmarked on my list.

Now that the year was coming to an end it was impossible for a movie role with Mohanlal to materialize. And lo! I got a call for a role in the film *Bhagwan*, starring none other than Mohanlal, to be shot with the aim of securing a Guinness World Record for being filmed in twenty-four hours. The shoot date was 10 December, and I had combination scenes only with the actor!

During the filming, Mohanlal suggested I read a book by Osho, titled *The Book of Secrets*. It was a series of discourses on *Vigyan Bhairav Tantra*, an ancient Indian text written over 5000 years ago and considered by many as the only book on meditation.

This book was a turning point of my identification as a powerful attracter to transitioning myself internally as an **instrument of higher consciousness**. From 'life is happening for me' to 'life is happening through me'. At this stage Consciousness identifies as the mind and the experience of power.

> *'When you change the way you look at things, the things you look at change.'*
>
> —*Wayne Dyer*

7

The Instrument

(I am the body–mind, in service of a higher power.)
Life is happening through me.

'If you really want something the whole universe
conspires to achieve it through you.'

—Lenaa

Trivandrum, 2009

The raindrops caught the city lights in them before falling off the balcony railings. A new hope and freshness were growing in me after a long time. The heavy book lying open in my lap had become my constant companion, lover, guru and my whole world. Its name, *The Book of Secrets: 112 Meditations to Discover the Mystery Within*—discourses by Osho on the ancient text of *Vigyan Bhairav Tantra.*

This rainy evening, back from filming for the day, freshly showered and ready to learn the sixth Sutra (technique) I read: **'Devices to Transcend Dreaming.'**

The device was to fix a subject in mind, while in meditation, and to dream about it while sleeping that night. I decided to visualize Osho in my dream and subsequently I would know it was a dream when he appeared in it. But as I tried to do this, a long black and orange snake appeared in my mind's eye. I wondered why, and stopped meditation and went straight to bed.

Dark, blankness. I was eight years old and asleep on a mat on the floor next to my mother and baby sister. A black and orange patterned snake slithered towards us from the far end of the dimly lit room of my mother's house.

In the dream, I recognized the snake! At that very instant, the dream's location shifted to my bedroom in Trivandrum where I lay asleep, and the snake began to move towards the bed I was physically sleeping on. It felt so real. (The hallmark of a lucid dream is that it takes place in the exact location in which the dreamer is physically sleeping, making it hard to distinguish from reality. Hence the term Lucid). The snake moved closer and was crawling up the bed towards my feet. In a sudden flash, I remembered the dialogue from Richard Linklater's film *Waking Life*, 'You cannot change the lighting in a lucid dream.'

The black snake was almost near my feet as I pushed the light switch next to the bed. It felt like a doorbell. It just wouldn't stay pressed and flipped back like a spring. I knew it was a dream, but I couldn't wake up! As I kept frantically pressing the light switch, it flicked ON! I woke up! The snake didn't exist!

I wiped the sweat off my brow, laughing in relief. That moment, the realization of the difference between deep sleep, dreaming and waking, which I had just experienced first-hand hit me! The three states of being.

However, it was only in June 2020 during a twenty-one-day solitary retreat that I remembered the key point in the lucid dream experience of 2009. That I am not the one deep in sleep or the dreamer or the awake person. I am the unmanifest witness that saw all three states that night.

True liberation is this identification with the fourth (*thuriya*)—'the witness'.

This moment manifests at its own pace and time. When the mind is ripe, it falls off, and with it, the Ego. This is the defining moment from whence all of life can only be seen as the ultimate lucid dream.

Imagine experiencing the spinning totem at the climax of the Christopher Nolan movie *Inception*. That moment when you know by experience that there is no such thing called reality—and that all manifest life is an illusion. What ancient Indians called Maya. What one calls One's Body–Mind is just a part of that grand dream being dreamt by the absolute consciousness, Life Itself, that one truly is.

From that moment in 2009, I identified the body–mind as one complementary expression and tool of God for experiencing and expressing the Self. I felt like saying, 'Thy will be done' or all is done 'God willing'.

Life went on . . .

8

The Creator (I Am Life)

Ahambrahmasmi (Sanskrit)—I am the All-Pervading Self.

A monk asked Lao Tzu, 'Why do you teach, "Mind is Buddha?"'

Lao Tzu replied, 'To stop a baby from crying.'

The monk said, 'When the crying has stopped, what then?'

Lao Tzu said, 'Then I teach, not mind, not Buddha.'
The monk asked, 'How about someone who is not attached to either?'

To which Lao Tzu answered, 'I would tell him not to be.'

So, the monk Inquired, 'And what if you met a man not attached to all things?'

Lao Tzu said, 'I would just let him experience the great Tao.'

—*Tao Te Ching*

The only obstacle to entering this stage of consciousness is knowledge.

If you think you know, you will miss the experience. These spontaneous moments of waking up will keep knocking at our hearts. It is a mind that is full and busy that stands in the way of waking up the inner wisdom. All said and done, everyone wakes up in his/her own time, in accordance with the grand design of things. Beginning to glimpse the grand design is synchronicity. As one of my professors in college, Dr Moncy Edward, loved saying, 'What, when, when, when happen; that, that, then, then, happen, happen.' It means everything happens exactly when it is meant to happen.

If you have read so far, you now have a definite answer to the question **'What am I?'**

As we saw previously, when we say, 'My body, my mind.' Who is claiming ownership? Everyone answers: 'I am.'

Then wonders, 'What am I?'

The direct question would be: **What is I?**

The direct answer: **I is Life.** 'I' that is also a number, a letter and a word means One, Self, Life. I = God.

This is why we all call ourselves I.

I am not the body, I am not the mind. I am the one who owns them.

I am the One that owns or rather expresses my-Self in all forms.

I am All.

All forms are expressions of I.

Knowing this answer is Self-Realization, Waking up, and Enlightenment!
Congratulations!

This coming full circle happened to me on 31 January 2018, in Kochi, Kerala.

As I stood alone on the terrace of my house watching the super-blood moon go into total eclipse, the still small voice in the meditative silence said, 'All I have to do is acknowledge that I am awake. No one else can do that for me.'

I did.

It had only been a month since I had stopped taking the psychiatric prescription medication that I had been on for fourteen years.

9

'God': Cause of All the Trouble

'I know that I exist; the question is, what is this "I" that "I" know?'

—Rene Descartes

Had I not used the word 'God' while explaining my experience in 2004, I would not have got into all the trouble that I did.

Having quit psychiatric medication and battled with the withdrawal symptoms (that are often looked upon as symptoms of illness and not withdrawal from medication), I decided to do something I had wanted to do all my adult life. In the spring of 2018, I tonsured my head and booked a one-way ticket to Kathmandu, Nepal. All I wanted was to be in the Himalayas, far away from everyone I knew and everyone who knew me.

I had expected to reach absolute clarity in the Himalayas. As I summited the Thorang La pass, after a fourteen-day trek in the Annapurna circuit, a sense of calm and reason welled in me. After roaming aimlessly in the Himalayas for two whole months, I returned to Kerala, a confident and clear-headed person. Or so I thought at the time.

> *'Reason has always existed in the world. But not in a reasonable way.'*
>
> —*Karl Marx*

It was a scorching-hot afternoon in the month of May 2022. The great Indian summer. My head felt like molten lava as I lay in bed with a migraine worse than anything I had ever experienced. By now, I knew that migraines, unexplainable by modern medicine, are in reality a huge vibrational realignment to new information that would change one's whole perspective.

The mind being expanded is painful. The resistance from the habitual mind causes migraine. So, I waited with a splitting head for the information to download from God into my mind.

The information came in the form of the words '*God is Atheist*'. The molten lava of my brain swirled in my head and I felt nauseated as these words started to make sense.

The questions began: *'When I say, "My body?" "My mind?" who is claiming ownership of the body and mind?'*

Until then, I thought the answer was 'I' and that the word 'I' meant God. I had believed this since that fateful day in 2004.

The information continued to pour into my mind.

'God does not exist.'

The migraine got worse.

'So, what is God?' I thought.

The answer came immediately, *'A human term that confuses and creates a mental block for an otherwise simple realization. Everything humans call God is something we know directly. It is LIFE.'*

'LIFE is GOD!'

'The complication begins when we start to believe that something Omnipresent, Omniscient, Omnipotent, Eternal and Infinite could have been created when it cannot be destroyed!

'Life does not know death. Hence, Life has no creator that can be called God!

'And every one of us, all the life forms know Life directly!'

This information blew my mind wide open, and the migraine was gone.

It was followed by stillness and clarity that came from demystifying the answer to *'What am I?'*

The simple answer: *'I am Life'*.

God = Life = I.

It began to rain outside and within me.

Aham Brahmasmi to *Brahmaivaham*.

From 'I am the Absolute' to 'The Absolute is all'.

Waking up is not the final destination, though. Life goes on purging levels of imbalance between the body–energy–mind until the very last identification with the personal self (form) transcends into pure Self (Life).

One Life, many bodies.

The identification at this state is 'I am the all-pervading self'—*Aham Brahmasmi* (Sanskrit).

10

Bliss Embodied (I Am Bliss)

The highest and subtlest stage of misidentification is 'I Am Bliss'. This identification too dissolves into pure consciousness after the initial flood of Bliss caused by love in the heart settles in and becomes the new normal. What remains is non-identification. This can only be experienced and not spoken or written nor understood because it's beyond comprehension but can be lived.

'Tat - twam - asi' (Sanskrit)
'That - you - are'

The sense of Self having journeyed through all the five stages of consciousness now stands reflecting itself like parallel mirrors. Consciousness, conscious of itself.

This identification moves one level further to overcome the premise that God is the all-pervading self, and instead a simple and egoless understanding that life is all there is (Brahmaivaham), which occupies the entire being.

The Aham (sense of self) dissolves in Brahman as the final realization of Brahmaivaham (Sanskrit).

Brahmaivaham = That is all that exists.

CONSCIOUSNESS

WHO AM I?

1

Who I Am

'The question "Who am I?" is not really meant to get an answer.
The question, "Who am I?" is meant to dissolve the questioner.'
                                                   —Ramana Maharshi

The dissolving that Ramana Maharshi speaks of is the mind and body surrendering to I/Life and becoming the tools for Life to experience and express It-Self.

Now that we know the answer to the question **What am I?**

We are Self-Realized.

The next question is: **Who am I?**

Self-Realization and Self-Actualization are two very different aspects.

Self-Realization is an instant spark of realizing or knowing what happens in the mind. It is an Aha! moment. That 'I hope' you had in the previous section.

Self-Actualization is acting out on what One knows. This must happen in the physical world, through the body.

Literally, Walking the Talk. Who I am is who I show up as in the world from moment to moment.

The difficulties faced in actualizing what is known are in rewriting the subconscious programming that had happened to the mind when One wasn't aware of What one is. That faulty premise, based on ignorance, is the ego. The ego comes from the reflective nature of the mind. The mind's nature is to behave like a mirror reflecting whatever it faces.

When the mind faces the physical reality, it reflects it as 'I am the world'.

When the mind faces the divine/Spiritual it reflects the meaning of Life. It begins to search for the meaning of Life.

I am Life, but, what is life? In the words of those who have known the meaning of Life, the mind knows it is CONSCIOUSNESS BLISS. To know and live according to One's knowing is to be free of the ego.

Now that **I know What I am . . . I have to recreate Who I am.**

Consciousness is the sea; mind is the wave of it.

Mind is the wave; thought is the shape of it.

Thought is the shape, it shapes the earth.

The earth turns into the world.

Personality: The outward expression of the totality of the individual mind's understanding of the nature of Life.

What the mind identifies with, it behaves as, through the body, in the world.

A mind that thinks it is attached to the body feels like a victim. A mind that thinks it is the supreme power that decides and does all things feels like a creator.

The mind that thinks it is an instrument of a higher power, that it does not know the nature of, feels like an instrument.

The mind that thinks it is an instrument of the higher and indestructible force of Consciousness feels Bliss.

What the mind feels is expressed as Personality or WHO I AM.

Who I am is how I show up in the world. Put simply, Who I am is how I behave on a consistent basis. Core Values are derived from what the mind identifies as. Core Values determine behaviour and hence Who I am.

To know yourself as you are now, take a few minutes to note down your own evaluation of yourself in some broad areas of life and then we can check which level of consciousness you are functioning at. Rate yourself on a scale of 10 on some broad areas of life which are given below:

#1 Health_____
#2 Fitness_____
#3 Intellectual_____
#4 Emotional_____
#5 Spiritual_____
#6 Friendships_____
#7 Family_____
#8 Love relationship_____
#9 Career_____

#10 Finance_____
#11 Travel and adventures_____
12 Environments_____
#13 Luxuries_____
#14 Desires_____
#15 Contribution to the world_____

The mind's core beliefs on all these areas and more comprise **Who I am.**

The liberating fact is knowing that one may be at a very high level of consciousness in one area while at the lowest level in other areas. Just become aware, and don't judge. I personally used areas I was strong in to aid in building up the ones I was weak in. The aim is to stabilize all areas at the highest possible rating. To show up in the world as One's Best Version. The best version of one functions with full consciousness in every area.

2

Roles

'We know what we are, but know not what we may be.'
—William Shakespeare

The Daughter

One afternoon, when I was four years old, I found a diary to scribble in. Overjoyed, I flipped through the empty pages that were all mine now. When I came to the last page my eyes widened, I felt my heart thumping in my little chest and a strange feeling of smallness begin to engulf me like a cold cloud. I was looking at the world map for the first time. It scared me for some reason unknown to me. Vague feelings of being so tiny and knowing so little while being in a world that is so huge and unfathomable made my small knees tremble. I shut the diary and sat in panic waiting for my father to return from the office. As soon as the doorbell rang, I ran up to him frantically and asked, 'Daddy! What is the difference between the world and the earth?' He noticed my pale, worried face and took me in his arms saying, 'The earth is a planet. The mud, the trees and all of nature. The world is all that human beings have made on earth.' A warm hug and a kiss after this beautiful explanation soothed my panic and I was the happy, mischievous and curious child again.

Being the firstborn to parents in their early twenties, I had a brilliant childhood and grew up with a lot of attention and encouragement. When my younger sister was born six years after me, I discovered unconditional love. Making my parents and everyone around me proud of me was a top priority for the achiever and perfectionist that I was. This made me quite a well-conditioned people-pleaser. I had always felt out of place everywhere, as though I needed to make an extra effort to fit in. All of this kept my true nature hidden within me.

As I write about this memory, I realize that what really frightened the four-year-old was not the size of the world, but rather the illusory nature of it. Perhaps this was the beginning of the search for the meaning of the world, what it is and where it comes from.

This confusion common to all human minds is cleared conclusively if the mind understands Adi Shankaracharya's teachings or for that matter any teachings from Advaita Vedanta.

To put it in the simplest possible words, the world is a projection of the mind on to the all-pervading canvas of Consciousness.

Consciousness being the very nature of Life.

The Actress

'People talk about the suspension of disbelief that you ask of the audience. Before that starts, you have to, as an actor, suspend your own disbelief.'

—**Helena Bonham Carter**

One warm afternoon on the Hari Sri Vidya Nidhi school campus in Thrissur, in 1998, the peon walked into the eleventh-grade calculus class and the teacher announced, 'Lenaa, meet Nalini Miss in the room next to the principal's office.'

The relief of leaving calculus was drowned by my thoughts, 'Why would the founder principal of the school pull me out of a class right now? Have I done something wrong?'

It turned out that she was auditioning a few girls of my age group for a theatre company she was planning. There were a few unknown faces in the room. I have loved acting since I was three years old and I put my heart and soul into the audition. Later that week, I was informed that it was a mock audition for the producer and associate of director Jayaraj's film *Sneham,* to see if I was right for the role in the film.

The day I was selected to act in my first film was perhaps the most confusing day of my whole teenage years. I was sixteen. Like any teenager who has a boyfriend, I called him first to share the thrilling news. I picked up the landline and dialled with bated breath expecting huge congratulatory excitement as soon as I made my announcement. He picked up and I blurted straight out, 'I've been selected to act in a film!'

My head spun, and my heart broke into a million pieces as I heard him say, *'What?! Are you crazy? You're going to act in films? Do you have any clue what kind of industry it is? People will look down on you with disrespect. Just say no!'*

My parents, on the other hand, were overjoyed and excited at the movie offer and encouraged me. I was in absolute dismay. I wanted to act in films with all my heart but the people-pleaser in me was in a dilemma.

The advice my father gave me on that day changed the course of the rest of my life. He said, *'There are no free lunches. It is your life and I suggest you decide what to do only based on exactly what you want. Not what we, your parents or your boyfriend or anyone else wants.'*

This experience was perhaps the moment of realizing that 'with great freedom comes great responsibility'. This moment was the turning point of my life, when I felt like an individual for the first time and began taking decisions. It was also the moment when the question 'who am I?' first occurred to me.

'Who am I?' In this part of the story (1998 to 2001), I'm a good student, a troubled teenager and a busy actress. I became a part of the film industry on 11 February 1998.

Four years and nine films later, graduating with a state rank in psychology, I decided to leave cinema and study to become a clinical psychologist.

The Clinical Psychologist

'There are two kinds of people in this world: the diagnosed and the undiagnosed.'

The unspoken questions: 'Who am I?' and 'What is this world?' haunted the mind throughout my childhood and adolescence. When the choice of which subject to pursue for higher education arose, it was by sheer divine intervention that I found out that a degree in psychology was an option.

The mind loved learning about itself. This love for the subject made it easy to pursue education alongside the acting career and excel at both.

Graduating as a state-level topper from Calicut University, Kerala, the decision for the next phase of life came as a surprise to everyone, including me.

I chose to leave cinema and join SNDT University, Mumbai, for a master's degree in clinical psychology.

In 2002, I wore a white doctor's coat and sat at the table assigned to me at JJ Hospital, Mumbai. Even before the butterflies in my stomach could settle, Jagath (name changed) sat down before me with the most melancholic vibe. Five years of theoretical learning does not prepare you for your first day of internship as a clinical psychologist.

Jagath was withdrawn, and responded quietly when I asked him questions repeatedly. He was brought for psychiatric help because although he was a postgraduate, he did not work and preferred to stay in his room at home, sitting in silence all day. He ate if he was given food. He kept his body clean and showed no signs of agitation. He showed no sexual interest in his wife, though he was kind and considerate to her.

Clinical evaluation required a battery of tests to be completed. All required long questionnaires to be filled out. As I asked Jagath question after question and recorded his answers, test after test, day after day, I lost my appetite, my sleep and all peace of mind. Checking and rechecking the final diagnosis that showed up as 'Paranoid Schizophrenia' did not change the verdict of the test results. I kept thinking, 'The tests are designed to give results of mental instability. You cannot take any psychological test and come out perfectly sane, even if you cheated.'

I couldn't help feeling heavy and wrong about the whole thing. Submitting the diagnosis to the psychiatrist who was in charge, I hoped with all my heart that he would do an expert re-evaluation. Deep down I consoled myself that the ordeal was over and that the next day at the hospital would be better.

Just then all the interns were called for rounds of the in-patient wards. The heavy metal trap doors, like the ones in jails, were the first startling sight. The chaos and stink of the dismal ward made me want to cry.

Our chief doctor told us that it was only the white coat we wore that protected us from an attack and that we were to be vigilant. Before those words settled in, a big guy came running towards me and stood inches from my face with a big grin on his face. I couldn't breathe. My eyes were wide as he pointed at a gap between his front teeth and asked me to get it closed.

The amused male attendant took him away and I almost ran to join the rest of the interns at the women's ward. A shiver ran up my spine as I saw the feces and menstrual blood rubbed on the walls. My eyes scanned the multiple beds with women of all ages. A beautiful girl, who looked like she came from a well-to-do family, told me with tears in her eyes, 'I feel like eating bun and chai. So bad *na?*' This experience was all I needed to realize I had no future in this line of work.

For five years, I had worked hard so that '*who I am*' would be a clinical psychologist instead of a film actress. Now as I lay in bed dreading the next morning at the hospital, I realized that leaving cinema had been an arrogant mistake and that being a sensitive artist at heart I couldn't take the pressures of being a psychologist. I lay awake all night staring at the darkness, which felt like my future.

I had never understood the word 'empathy' until that particular day. As I sat dazed and confused at my table in the hospital, Jagath was rolled past me on a gurney to the ECT (electroconvulsive therapy) room. As he passed my desk, he held me in a blank stare. I felt the cold sharp stab of guilt. I sat transfixed in my chair as the heavy door closed and the hazard light turned on. Time seemed to have stopped. The creaky wheels of the gurney rolled back out of the ECT room.

I had to look. Spit dripping from the side of his mouth, Jagath's glazed and teary eyes still stared at me as they rolled him back out. The air was too heavy to breathe. Guilt, self-doubt, fear and loathing became me. Just then the next patient was brought in.

A young girl, brought by her mother and sister, sat down in front of me. I was shaking from head to toe as I asked them to wait and said that I'd send someone else. I ran up to a fellow intern and asked her to attend to the new patient.

I picked up my mobile phone to call home and to cry and confess to my parents that they were right. That I shouldn't have chosen clinical psychology and that I shouldn't have left my film career at its height.

Just then the phone in my hand rang. Startled, I answered the call.

The voice at the other end said, 'Hi! Is this Lenaa? I'm calling regarding a film named *Koottu* and want to know if you would play the leading lady with Aravind. We start filming in a week.'

I could have collapsed with relief.

Soon after, I became disillusioned with psychology and came back to cinema in 2003 with the film *Koottu*.

Yet, I quit acting again. This time to get married and start a whole new life.

The Wife

'An ideal wife is any woman who has an ideal husband.'
—**Booth Tarkington**

Though *Koottu* was my ticket out of psychology, my core was shaken up. I needed a place to hide away. I didn't want to live with my parents for my vanity's sake.

My boyfriend since age twelve, Abhilash was my only escape from reality. I left films and psychology, and prepared to be a full-time housewife.

On 16 January 2004, Abhi and I got married. I left my acting career once again. A tiny one-bedroom flat was all we could afford at that time. We lived on love, polluted Bangalore air and reckless escapist youthfulness. He worked hard at a call center with US work timings and I sat up all night watching Star Movies and HBO on a 16-inch television set. We slept all day, and on weekends we partied hard.

All this lasted from 16 January to the fateful day, 3 September 2004.

In December 2004, I valued the gift of acting more than ever, with my new beginning in television, with the series *Omanathingal Pakshi*.

What I had taken for granted now became a dream—to be back in the cinema.

I kept thinking . . . Who am I?

If I am not the roles I play in real life or on screen, who am I?

The medications and my preoccupation with getting well and actualizing what I had realized eventually saw us mutually agree to go our separate ways in 2010.

I'm glad we did that. That is why we continue to be good friends to date.

3

What I Am Is Not Who I Am

'Once upon a time, I dreamt I was a butterfly, fluttering hither and thither, to all intents and purposes a butterfly. I was conscious only of my happiness as a butterfly, unaware that I was myself. Soon I awoke, and there I was veritably myself again.

'Now I do not know whether I was then a man dreaming I was a butterfly, or now a butterfly dreaming I am a man.'

—*Zhuangzi (369-286 BCE)*

For someone devoid of feelings or rather incapable of knowing what I was feeling, because of constant psychiatric medication, being a professional actress was the absolute irony.

Acting was my therapy, my source of livelihood, my journey of self-discovery, my only passion and hope, and my meditation.

I was alive only in the moments between 'Action' and 'Cut'. I became a workaholic. I was blessed with great opportunities to act and great actors to work with and learn from. But inside I felt hollow and like an outsider. I was friends with everyone in the film industry. I saw them as my extended family. Yet I lacked the self-confidence and presence that actors usually exude. I was lost.

As I mentioned, it was Mohanlal who showed me the way forward. Noticing that I was reading a book called *Courage* by Osho, Lalettan (as we fondly call him) told me, 'If you are serious about transformation, read the *Vigyan Bhairav Tantra.*'

Apart from experiencing through that great book the lucid dream that life is, I also began to create **Who I am.**

To put it simply, Being Enlightened or Waking up or Realizing the nature of the Self only makes One lighter within, but not necessarily effective in the world.

Being Life and Living effectively require focusing on **How One shows up in the world from moment to moment.**

This requires grounding and purpose and vision and above all . . . Desire!

Since this phase of learning from the *Vigyan Bhairav Tantra,* I stopped identifying myself with the roles I played and the world around me seemed to transform every day.

I stopped seeing myself as a person and rather saw my-Self as an energy field of Consciousness that was driven by Desire.

4

Need. Want.
Desire.

A major side effect of Self-Realization is the loss of any need, want or desire due to the experience of One-Self as all-there-is!

Many have stopped at that level of mind where logic and reason become unnecessary.

This is where I am grateful to my family and friends for putting me in psychiatric care. Due to this, Desire could arise once again, and I am living out my potential rather than wandering as a bliss bunny!

As long as one is in a body on earth and identified with the body, the experience is always 'duality'.

That of knowing I am One and whole, Infinite and Eternal and yet experiencing my-Self as separate and individual, finite and mortal.

Mastering this balancing act is the **Mastery of Life.**

In the rest of this book, I will share with you all the techniques and tools I used to balance duality and reach a high integration of Conscious and Subconscious, Body and Mind, Energy and Consciousness.

Some basics first:

Need signifies the lack of something.

Want signifies the choice to have something.

Desire signifies a deep wanting, hopefulness and wishfulness with the added emotion of longing and imagination of having it.

The Paradigm Shift of Desire

Where does desire come from?

Putting aside the commonly believed idea that desire arises from within the mind, let us look at **desire as a command** to achieve or create or experience something, coming into the mind, in the form of vibrations, from the unknown or rather from the I/Life, and being translated by the intellect as an idea that then becomes a desire, that is then sent as an impulse in the body to *Do* something.

This paradigm takes away all the stress of having chosen a particular decision and instead the mind is able to focus on the task that it has been entrusted with by Consciousness/ I/Life.

This leads to a clear alignment of body, mind and I.

I/Consciousness/Life gives a command to the mind that appears as a desire, which then prompts action from the body so that the being, moves towards achieving that desire which leads to the experience that I wants the mind to have, so as to break the identification of I with body/mind/intellect.

Every true, deep and intrinsic desire one feels is a command from Life itself to this mind so that the body may *do* what is needed for Life to experience itself, as Consciousness Bliss.

Desire vs Need

If you find yourself living in a box of needs, then you are in one of the boxes in Abraham Maslow's pyramid of needs.

Pyramid of Needs

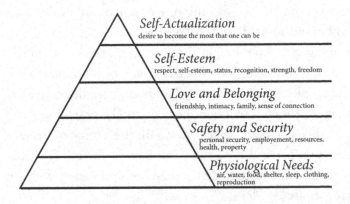

Self-Actualization
desire to become the most that one can be

Self-Esteem
respect, self-esteem, status, recognition, strength, freedom

Love and Belonging
friendship, intimacy, family, sense of connection

Safety and Security
personal security, employment, resources, health, property

Physiological Needs
air, water, food, shelter, sleep, clothing, reproduction

Figure 4: Maslow's Hierarchy of Needs

One must have a clear idea of one's needs. However, desire is the thing that makes one get out of bed in the morning (especially, to go to work). To beat depression, one must desire something.

The desire for self-esteem is a paradox. We try to impress others with our material possessions and with how worthy they should think we are of their holding us in high esteem when the very need is for **self-esteem,** which only you can give to yourself.

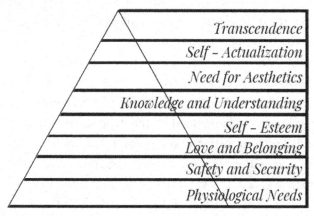

Figure 5: An expanded version of the Hierarchy of Needs model

Two modern-day issues with this area are:

1. Self-esteem is confused with social standing or status. This has to do with borrowed desires. They are the root of all misery. You can never enjoy their fruit, because the seed wasn't yours, to begin with. If social media or peer pressure is the source of your desires in life, anxiety, stress and depression come free with it.

2. Not knowing what you truly want. Unless you take time with yourself to cut out everyone else's desires that are filling you, your true desires will not surface.

They are buried somewhere deep down along with your childhood memories.

While biological and psychological needs demand their fulfilment rather drastically, aesthetic needs are just as painful as all others when unfulfilled. Here, the dilemma is that it doesn't look as important as a need, but it is an overwhelming personal need.

The desire for creativity, freedom and expressing authenticity and knowing the truth is the highest of human needs. Existential angst and the heights of anxiety about the unknown accompanied by the depression of not fitting in, not knowing how to evolve, confusion about truth and searching, without knowing what for, are the hallmarks of this stage. It is at this stage of our desire for deeper meaning that we feel most alone and at times lonely. This stage of anxiety and depression is a luxury. You get here only when the other levels of needs are satisfied and not escaped. Congratulate yourself if you are at this stage because *desire* takes on a whole new meaning from here.

Waking up to the meaning of desire from this stage we see it as a sign or force that rises within us to propel us in the direction of evolution, truth and destiny. Like all pure creativity, desire comes from a source beyond our limited perceptions of self. Then desire is seen as the fuel to unleash one's true and individual potential.

Desires are signs that lead to higher synchronicities, showing us the way to our higher self.

Then one sees that the universe is planting a desire in one's heart to manifest that through one. And what you desire is desiring you.

These desires lead to a legacy. They are always service- or contribution-oriented and contain the reward in the very unfoldment of the desire. Every step of making that desire come true has immense joy and contentment in it and gifts it all around.

Desirelessness or being conscious and knowing oneself as the infinite void is the last stage of consciousness development in human beings.

Desirelessness does not, however, mean apathy, laziness or inactivity. It is a state of knowing oneself as the witness of all desire and doing, even while the body–energy–mind that realizes this, continues to do its work, through feeling desire and acting upon it.

Writing this book is one such activity that the intellect, mind and body are involved in. However, the book is only intended to share the practical aspects of waking up to one's true nature as Life–Consciousness–Bliss.

5

Consciousness

If the reader has become conscious of the nature of self, many questions regarding the technical aspects of consciousness will arise in the mind.

Until now, the mind most probably thought consciousness is a quality of the mind.

Now, when aware that awareness/consciousness is the prerequisite for thinking, feeling and perceiving, which is the mind, the mind gets disturbed. Thinking, feeling and perceiving increase.

This is when to remember that I am consciousness aware that the mind is disturbed and is trying to rearrange everything it thinks it knows based on this new information.

In reality, what is happening is that the mind's capacity for logical storage of information is going through a complete rearrangement.

This rearrangement from the point of view of consciousness is called evolution through paradigm shifts.

The rearrangement in the mind's storing system into new logical patterns from the mind's point of view is chaos. (Like the shifting or rearrangement of a house, or even a messy cupboard.)

Since the mind that is going through the process of logic rearrangement, to the body and other bodies, it seems to be illogical or in simple words insane.

When the insanity has begun with clear information about the nature of self, it is more peaceful and organized.

This organized rearrangement of mind is the journey from Self-Realization to Self-Actualization.

Although it sounds simple to say the journey from self-realization to self-actualization is the rearrangement of the entire mind, when experienced by the mind, it is like lifting oneself up by one's own shoelaces. The mind has to work on itself. And anything the mind does, reflects as behaviour through the body.

This is why, the mind trying to rearrange itself needs the wisdom of minds that have already done this job. Those who have undertaken this huge constant uphill climb of a journey have always left ropes or signs along the way for future travellers. They are left in the form of written or spoken words.

Only words can reach troubled minds that are on the arduous journey of rearranging their logic till the realization that began in the mind is experienced in the body. These words that help troubled minds make sense of the world— by dispelling the mind's misconceptions—are like water to one dying of thirst. The searching mind will always find the words of a mind similar to it, one that has completed the journey. Those great minds will seem relatable, while other great minds' words may not.

Once begun, the mind will rest only when everything makes perfect logical sense.

For the mind writing this book, the great words that helped it reach perfect logic come from the school of Advaita Vedanta. To be specific, the process that began with the words in the *Vigyan Bhairav Tantra* ended with the words from *Vivekachudamani*, by Adi Shankaracharya.

As the saying goes, 'When the student is ready, the master appears.'

Dear reader,

Keep rearranging the logic in the mind until it reaches one unified whole of wisdom. Do not stop when there are still compartments in the mind.

A unified mind will experience beyond the words, the truth held within them.

A mind that has completed its work rests not in mere peace but in something only such a mind can know—Bliss!

BLISS

WHERE, WHEN AND WHY AM I?

1

Being the Best Version of I

'Who I am is the personification of what I am.'

—Lenaa

A friend once asked me, 'Why is it that you could not explain what you had realized when it happened in 2004, and how come you can explain it so easily now?'

I laughed and replied, 'We didn't all have smartphones then!'

The Smartphone Example (Highly Simplistic)

If the **hardware** of the smartphone is '**My Body**', the **software** of the smartphone is '**My Mind**'. The **charge** in the battery is '**My Energy**'. The **Internet** that makes the phone 'smart' would be **'consciousness'**, not 'my' consciousness because it doesn't belong to the phone and is non-local.

The One aware of all of this is *consciousness*, that would be *you* or rather 'I'.

My friend liked the analogy and said, 'Wow! But really does it take that long . . . like nineteen years . . . to get from realization to actualization?'

I knew this demanded a detailed explanation. So here it is:

Due to the fact that in order to explain the journey from Self-Realization to Self-Actualization many esoteric experiences will need to be shared and they would not be of use or may even be misleading to a reader who is before the stage of Self-Realization, I will not mention them in this book. However, I will share here some events that occurred, that may contain tools for the reader.

1. I had been on psychiatric medication which caused numbness of the psyche and emotions. Evolution for me only began manifesting after I stopped taking the medication on my own responsibility in 2017. *(Please do not stop your medication or treatment without consulting your doctor.)*

2. An Access Consciousness Bars energy healing session in 2017, by my friend Anushree Nair, had opened up stagnant energy pathways that allowed blocked emotions and capabilities to emerge and be healed.

3. My body had gone through a complete overhaul in 2020 with four months of Ayurvedic Panchakarma, cleansing and treatment, including rejuvenation of damaged neural and energetic (nadi) pathways, at

Ayurveda Yoga Villa, Wayanad, a place in the forest by the Kabini River, Kerala.

4. I had my spinal alignment done using Marmam (traditional Indian skeletal realignment method) and Dorn treatment. Apparently, if your upper spinal disks are not aligned with your skull, you remain stuck in intellectualization, unable to materialize your thoughts. Every disk in your spinal cord, if not in its exact position, creates severe physical and mental symptoms due to the less obvious imbalance in energy flow. (See table of spinal correlate.)

5. I had then spent twenty-one days in absolute solitude with no stimulation of any of my five senses. That included being alone without books, music or any digital medium, and the repetitive taste of one form of rice porridge (sattvic food), and just a small oil lamp to light the room.

6. I came out of the solitary treatment ready to write this book. The title, *The Autobiography of God,* and the five W's appeared to me in meditative clarity. I had promised to myself in 2017 that I would write about the ways that I had used to come out of the label and the psychiatric medicines that were thrust upon me if I could stay stable and aware of my truth for two years. It's now five years!

7. The earth's vibrational frequency has shifted from three-dimensional to five-dimensional since 2012, coinciding with the end of the Mayan calendar and the beginning of the shift in polarities. This makes all

consciousness on earth more aware and awake and it has been evolving since.

8. The *Age of Information* is transmuting into the *Age of Enlightenment* where spontaneous realizations and communication about enlightened topics become more possible.

9. Now, more than ever, humankind needs to wake up in a hurry before AI (artificial intelligence) catches us napping.

10. Timing is everything. Timing is the synchronized harmony of life forms and events. This perfection is what we call destiny or the will of life/I. Since everyone is the ultimate self, everyone feels like there is free will. This free will is known only on reaching Self-Actualization. A glimpse of the precision of timing can be known through Vedic astrology and other Vedic sciences. By the time I complete writing this book that began in 2020, it is July 2023. I realize that in Vedic astrology the period of nineteen years has special significance marked by two months of Shravan that occur once every nineteen years. It is also the time taken to complete one full cycle of the planetary motions from where they began on one's birth chart. The experience of Self-Realization that began on 3 September 2004 reaches full blossom and can be shared in words by September 2023. That makes it nineteen years. 2023 also makes twelve years of living alone. In Indian Vedic sciences, this period of twelve years also has special significance.

11. When the individual Intellect is in sync with destiny, the mind and body are under the control of consciousness/ life, and not the ego. Knowing that I am life means the body, mind, intellect and energy are under the surveillance of consciousness; this is pure Bliss.

12. The realization of **Why I Am** here now as Lenaa, that my life's purpose is to share this information with all that would benefit from it. So that I may spare you years of seeking and the struggles of the 'dark night of the soul'. So that you may be able to fast-forward into the pursuit of creating 'who you want to be' and enjoy a full and satisfying lifetime of expressed potential.

2
Where Am I?

'Logic will get you from A to B. Imagination will take you everywhere.'

—*Albert Einstein*

The Logic from A to B

Where am I? = I am where I know Myself.

Where I don't know myself, only Mind (thinking, feeling, experiencing) exists. Knowing is the nature of I. I am sentience. Am consciousness without which even thinking is impossible.

For example, when one faints, it is loss of consciousness which is a temporary death. The body and mind are not functioning, only the energy flow continues. If the consciousness is not restored soon, the flow of energy too will stop. That is why a body–mind in coma is sustained only through an artificial supply of energy.

This brings up the question:

What is energy?

Energy is the counterpart or part and parcel of Consciousness. Energy is the subtlest form of consciousness. It appears to make things move or function. Depending upon the level of Consciousness associated with the Energy is its Intelligence.

Energy is Consciousness in motion.

When it moves at the least possible pace, it is Meditation.

Energy and Consciousness cannot be created or destroyed. They are the nature of Life.

I am Life.

Imagination

A presence in the room.

Just as one is dozing off to sleep there is sometimes the feeling of falling or of an unknown presence in the room. This is the closest experience of God/Consciousness in situations other than meditation.

Sleep is nothing but the slight withdrawal of consciousness from the physical body. Consciousness moves out a safe enough distance to keep the body functioning but not awake. It is at this point of deep nervous relaxation that—due to ignorance of the nature of consciousness or how it orchestrates sleep and waking—the mind (ego) projects a story of an evil presence lurking or ghosts.

There is only one presence. It is Life/Consciousness/God/I.

Close your eyes and check where you *feel* yourself to be. (Do this before reading further.) Think 'Where am I?'

Despite the exact location, say, on your sofa, in a room in a building, in a compound, in a district of a state, in a country, in the world, on planet earth, in this solar system, in the universe, one has a distinct experience of being somewhere.

The experience of 'right here in my body' or 'everywhere' to anywhere in between these two. This personal sense of existing changes depending on which dimension of reality 'I' choose to perceive.

In the **body-mind** or **space-time** three-dimensional reality, 'I' focuses on the material and all things known. In this 3D reality, time moves linearly through past–present–future. In this reality, lives the familiar and hence the future is just a projection of what I know. In short, I live in memory and keep strengthening it and I call it my comfort zone.

In the **mind-body** or **time-space** 5D reality 'I' focuses on the unfamiliar, abstract, energetic and conceptual. This opens unlimited possibilities and absolute dynamics living in the present moment because I am vulnerable and on an adventure. Time in this reality only relates to the present moment of *Now*.

This shift of focus and identification happens usually in extreme situations, say, when one is pushed into the present moment by an accident or a sudden unexpected miracle or when one falls in love or has near-death experiences. These moments are the narrow pathways that lead from the 3D way of perceiving to 5D living.

The most expansive experience of Oneself, however, is where 'I' feels fully present in the physical body and as an infinite expanse in all directions. This quantum experience of being the body (particle) and the energy (vibrations) simultaneously is possible only when the observer is observed and is the ultimate singularity.

To the question 'Where am I?' physical location, location in time (past, present, future), location of how far along to achieving my goals, location of me on an emotional scale and any other device of measurement are applicable. Seeing the infinite answers to this question shows us our true infinite potential.

All other locations are accessed while being 100 per cent present in one's physical body and expanding out in waves.

In the past nineteen years, I have travelled through various dimensions and explored as many phases and facets of Self/Life as I could as the ego called Lenaa.

These explorations of the details of Life are what make Being Alive the ultimate experience. The reason why infinite and formless Life/I associate with a finite form. It is only because of being in this association with finite form that explorations of dimensions from Physical, Ethereal, Astral, Mental, Spiritual/Occult, Cosmic and Infinite Nothing (*shunyata*) of nature are possible. In these realms, the added dimension of past, present and future times creates unending probabilities and possibilities. The fact to be remembered vividly during any experience is that 'I' am always only the witnessing consciousness, not the body, mind or intellect having the experience. The experience is an effect of previous actions alone.

To travel, explore and have adventures in as many dimensions as possible and to really celebrate your Self/Life on planet earth an Earth-Suit is absolutely compulsory! All exploration is only the mind wandering due to ignorance of what 'I' is.

3

The Earth-Suit

'Thanks to my finiteness, I know my infinity. Thanks to my mortality, I know my eternity.'

—***Lenaa***

The only way to have an experience of living on earth is for Life/I to be in an Earth-Suit. An Earth-Suit is the one and only tool that 'I' gets in a lifetime and it has three components (and many subtler divisions):

1. The physical body
2. The energy body
3. The mental body

The Neurology of 'What Am I?' and 'Who Am I?'

I realized a few things while watching a TED talk by Dr Jill Taylor, 'A Stroke of Insight':

1. This is exactly what happened to me on magic mushrooms and how lucky I am that I did not have to go through a stroke to have the exclusive right-brain experience.
2. Because she was a brain scientist, she invoked the experience of a stroke to understand how insight works on the inside of the brain and because I was a psychologist, I invoked the experience of how insight works inside the mind.
4. The psychological aftermath of the insight for me lasted fourteen years while she had the neurological aftermath of an insight which lasted eight years.
5. While Dr Jill learnt to train the whole brain to work together, I learnt to appease the rational mind with logical answers to illogical and mystical experiences which in turn led to whole mindfulness.

So, my major takeaway from Dr Jill Taylor's clarity on the hemispheres of the brain and their roles in real life is that the right hemisphere has the answers to 'What am I?' while the left hemisphere defines 'Who am I?'.

To have the expansive (right-brain) experiences of Being Consciousness one has to first approach the logical, rational left hemisphere (the gatekeeper) and sell the idea to it.

Once the logical brain has been addressed it allows the being to relax. Only in deep relaxation can Consciousness become conscious of itself or, in other words, can Self -Realization occur.

Self-Realization happens in the right hemisphere while the practical steps to actualization begin to happen in the left hemisphere of the brain. This realignment of the mind and brain takes time, which can be called its healing time after the traumatic event of realization. All through the healing, though, much of living occurs!

Physical

Being present in the Here–Now is to be fully aware of One's physical form with the mind and energy focused on the consciousness of the physical. Such a person is extremely powerful and is said to have a great presence, presence of mind, which is attractive and highly effective in the world.

To be fully present in the body, walk barefoot on the earth for some time or visualize an earthing cable connecting you to the earth, through the feet and at the root (earth) *chakra* at the base of the spine. Sitting on the floor or directly on the earth or on rocks is great too. These practices are called grounding or earthing. This will allow you to be 'here', whether your mind is in the now or not.

The first time I did this visualization exercise we are about to embark upon was life-changing! Let's dive straight into it.

Sit comfortably with your back as straight and relaxed as possible. Keep your hands in your lap or on your knees. Close your eyes and take a few focused deep breaths. Now visualize roots coming out of the base of your spine. (Continue reading after doing the visualization.)

What did your roots look like?

When I first did the visualization, I had frail and pale-looking short roots connecting me to the ground. This was a clear sign of my lack of grounding. Another revealing trait I had of my lack of grounding was that I ate and walked extremely fast. I would finish a meal in less than five minutes!

Have you seen giant trees? Sturdy and tall with wide trunks and big wide branches? If you were to see the part of them under the soil or rather within the earth it would be just as large as the part out of the soil! Deep, wide, thick roots as heavy as the branches of the tree would be grounding it to the earth and feeding it nutrients and deeper communication with other trees and the planet itself.

If the roots you visualized were not as big as your physical body itself, how do you expect to feel grounded, safe, secure, worthy of being here, in control of your life, having self-confidence, etc., etc., etc.?

If you want to grow and evolve into a powerful and influential or impactful person, then don't you think the roots you visualize need to be as deep and strong?

If you want to have a global impact, must not your roots be inside the whole planet with you branching out across the earth and into the sky?

As I began visualizing massive roots, I began eating slower, walking with assured firm steps and speaking with calmness and command. I slept better and felt like I fitted in for the first time in this lifetime.

Energetic

Energy healers are an expression of Life in various forms varying from geographical locations, and healing plants to animals and birds, human beings, music, beings of light and beyond. All are particular vibrational frequencies of the same Life.

In July 2017, an energy healer, Anushree Nair, contacted me via Facebook Messenger, something I almost never checked. That particular day, I opened the Messenger inbox without any idea why I was doing it. I happened to open this message from her and in it, where she described an energy-healing modality called Access Consciousness Bars. I didn't have the faintest clue about energy healing at the time. The same intuition that made me check the message told me to do the session she was offering.

We scheduled a session and it felt very easy and relaxing, to say the least. Before she left, she gave me some simple instructions and said, 'It's best to just let the energy flow freely now that many blocks have been cleared; if you resist the change, you might get a headache. Don't worry it will clear up. Drink plenty of water and relax.'

A head-splitting migraine began soon after she left, and I remembered her telling me not to resist the shifts in energy, and I slept. The next day I woke up a totally different person. All the restrictions and limitations I had put upon myself as voluntary imprisonment had fallen away. Absolutely amazing clarity and confidence filled me. I then read a book called *The Other Side of Bipolar* by Lauren Polly, revealing your strengths to go beyond the diagnosis. I decided to stop taking medications for the sake of others' peace of mind.

Anushree is a good friend now and I'm thankful she introduced me to the magical world where energy is tangible without words or actions.

Mental

Most of us who have gone through anxiety or depression are highly sensitive to energies whether we know it or not. Knowing this makes us capable of dealing with it.

How did I deal with poor energy boundaries or lack of a clear and grounded personal space (empathy)?

By constantly remembering

1. What I am . . . is Life itself. 'Who am I?' is a constant creation, based on my choices.
2. 'Who am I?' does not have anything to hide, prove, protect or defend. Only to learn from feedback by contemplation and evolution based on what rings true for me.
3. There is no need to fear others' opinions since no one can control or coerce me into being anything other than myself. However, being able to listen to them without fear allows me the ability to heal anything in me that is in my blind spot (shadow self).
4. My personal space is sacred and only I have permission to alter it. All the space outside my personal space (the rest of the universe) is open ground for others and their points of view. This understanding allows me to be calm and receptive to myself while others express who they are.

5. Constantly being aware of one's personal space and keeping its boundaries clearly makes for comfortable communication.

6. Being in a mindset of non-judgemental allowance without agreeing or disagreeing is the sweet spot.

7. When I become aware of a previous limitation in me, I let go of it and grow and celebrate the moment.

8. Constant evolution of infinite consciousness through a finite form is who I am.

9. Yoga, qigong and crystals help set emotional and energetic boundaries.

10. We are all 'Unique Points of Experience' from where we have a 'Unique Point of View' of everything and nothing. Our uniqueness is in every one of us being a unique expression of the 'Whole of Life' while being 'All of Life' simultaneously.

> 'You are not a drop of the ocean. You are the whole ocean in a drop.'
>
> —*Rumi*

The ancient yogic and tantric view is that the microcosm or Earth-Suit, as I call it, is made up of everything from earth to the cosmos and is a representation of the:

Whole = everything + nothing.

Body	Energy	Mind
Skeletal alignment	Chakra alignment	Cognitive alignment
Muscle building	Energy boundaries	Clearing mental blocks and limitations
Healthy microbiome	Breathwork	Destroying old patterns of thinking, behaving and receiving
Clean nutrition	Yoga, tai chi, qigong, loving relations	Communication
Body awareness		Self-love
Loving the body		Belief systems
		Journaling
		Self-mastery classes

4

Self-Evaluation

To know *Where I am* in each area of Worldly Experience.

'When you love yourself, you love everyone and everything that happened to you, for they shaped the person you are now.'

—Lenaa

To love oneself requires one to know oneself. The broad areas one needs to know about oneself are:

1. What level of identification am I functioning at most of the time?

   a. Victim
   b. Attractor
   c. Instrument
   d. Being

2. What do I hate or love? They are clues to what I repress or deny.
3. How do I talk to myself?

   a. Critical
   b. Nurturing
   c. Conspiratory
   d. In the third person

4. What do I want from others I am in a relationship with?

   a. Approval
   b. Control
   c. Encouragement
   d. Support (emotional/financial)
   e. Love
   f. Judgement
   g. Others

5. Do I have anything to hide, prove, defend or protect?
6. What are the things, people or ideas I need to let go of and why?
7. What areas in life am I weak in and how can I educate myself there?
8. Do I love myself without judgement?
9. What type of person am I on various personality type scales? Take some online quizzes. For example:

   a.   16 PF
   b.   Sparkytype
   c.   Braintype
   d.   Archetypes

10. What am I passionate about?
11. What would I like to do to leave behind a legacy?

5

When Am I?

*'I will no longer mutilate and destroy myself in order to find
a secret behind the ruins.'*

—Hermann Hesse, Siddhartha

To the question **'When am I?'** there is no reference to the
relative concept of 'time'. The aspect of 'time' is absolutely
related to the 'Where am I?'. It is not a question of being
at the right time at the right place. It is a deep sense of
timelessness.

TIME = THE JOURNEY FROM IGNORANCE TO CONSCIOUSNESS

When in love, in nature, in peace, in meditation One knows
'When I am'. One experiences timelessness. This is the
state of a Self-Actualized One. Upon becoming conscious
of One's true nature, the ignorance ends and with it the
pressure of ignorance felt as the limitedness of time ends.

When is a deep experience of self-discovery. The only answer being 'I am Now'. Eternal.

'There will never be any more perfection than there in Now.'
—***Walt Whitman***

'At this moment, there is plenty of time. At this moment, you are precise as you should be. At this moment, there is an infinite possibility.'
—***Victoria Moran***

'Meditation is the only medicine.'
—***Osho***

Since you have read so far, you know by now that every autobiography is the autobiography of God. In fact, it is a 'Life Story: One of the Stories Life Lives Out.'

As I wrote about the past, I am right here now. Being present in the present moment watching the memories flash in the mind ready to be written about in the now. This clarity of being a detached witness of all things past and future is the *Now*. Whether you are remembering something (past) or imagining (the future) you can only do it while being 'Here–Now'.

I am not just present. I am presence. To appreciate this experience of 'When am I?' one practises meditation. A technique that is practised till one arrives at the state of meditation. Getting skilled at meditation techniques is only to get the knack of becoming the state of meditation.

Much like gaining cycle balance, it just clicks one day. In meditation, I am not the meditator meditating. I am meditation. Meditation is the effortless abidance in Self nature. A state of total all-inclusive presence. Non-judgemental allowance and knowing.

Are you ready to write your version of the autobiography of God?

6
Why Am I?

'Our own self-realization is the greatest service we can render the world.'

—*Ramana Maharshi*

Why am I (here)?

One evening, as I enjoyed picking my father's brains, while he was driving the car and I sat next to him, I asked him, 'Why do people have children?'

His answer that I did not understand fully that day but remember word for word was:

'Children are our genetic fingertips reaching for the stars.'

—*T. Mohan Kumar*

The meaning of these words dawned in full clarity when Lenaa stopped experiencing Self as a person and experienced it instead as Life.

The body that one experiences as being in and as, is a continuation of cellular activity from the beginning of cellular life and carries memories of the atomic, subatomic and pure 'nothingness' state.

The body carries all memories of everything. This is cellular ancestry. The obsessive urges within us at any given moment are the continuation of all desires of our ancestors that continue as the body. If these body urges are not under the control of consciousness, we feel pressed for time and unsure of our purpose. We end up confused and trying out all kinds of things as our ancestry tosses us like driftwood on a turbulent sea.

This ancestry of cellular memory is sometimes experienced as past-life memories. They are memories of the journey the genetic material has accumulated through interactions with other genetic material over the extended period of reproduction and interaction over generations.

We are all connected in physical, mental and energetic realms through the same consciousness that is manifest as life forms.

Why am I?

Since life cannot die, I am always existence. Life cannot die/end because it never began. This is known in heart by life, because of its nature of consciousness.

Life is conscious energy and consciousness and energy are without beginning and end.

I am this conscious energy called life that is conscious of itself.

I am self-actualized when I am always conscious that I am conscious energy and not the projections of the mind on I.

I am self-actualized when I am constantly aware that I am conscious energy called life and not the body–mind.

I am life alone.

I am conscious energy alone.

I am knowing that I am conscious energy through this body–mind.

I experience myself as love in the heart. The only purpose in being associated with a body–mind is to know myself.

To know what I am.

Why am I? $\xrightarrow[\text{To Experience}]{\text{To Know}}$ What am I?

And so the five questions, the five W's in this book have come full circle.

> 'The mystery of human existence lies not in just staying alive, but in finding something to live for.'
> —*Fyodor Dostoyevsky*

Knowing that **what I am** is omnipotent, omniscient, omnipresent, eternal and infinite life living in this finite form of **who I am** as a person in the **Here and Now** leads me to clearly know as a deep desire in my heart **why I am** here.

That *why* is so uniquely individual to each being that only you can find it in peaceful discovery. It is invariably something that you *desire*, you are *passionate* about; it is a *contribution* to others, and fills you with *satisfaction* even when you just think of it.

Everyone is whole and an integral part of the larger whole in an ever-expanding consciousness. This knowing is to exist as bliss. Do what you love and do it as a whole-hearted contribution of your having been a finite moment of the infinite and you are fulfilled.

> *'They also serve who only stand and wait.'*
> —*John Milton on his blindness*

In the grand design of the all-inclusive, nothing is an accident. So, if you are anxious and there is worry, it is just so that you may plan your next step.

If you genuinely desire, it shows you the way. If you are relaxed and easily in love with yourself, you are home.

This book is one of the reasons why I am here now as Lenaa.

Have you found your **why**?

Write your mission statement: I am here on earth so that I . . .

Remember to keep your thoughts light and fun. Being Life itself all you are doing is exploring and expressing yourself through this form. Live, love and celebrate!

7

The Paradox (Nothing Being Everything)

'Nothing ever is. Everything is becoming.'

—*Plato*

I had been doing a course offered by Chinmaya International Foundation on Shankaracharya's *Vivekachudamani*. It had a profound impact in organizing the lifetime of events that had occurred to me and that were being written in this book. I also had the good fortune of meeting Br Ved Chaitanya, who was teaching the course, when I visited the maternal home of Adi Shankaracharya.

The days after completing the *Vivekachudamani* were mystical. The mind was rapidly rearranging itself while also receiving new information downloads in sleep and waking.

I had retreated to absolute solitude and spiritual living. New routines formed on their own.

On 14 July 2023, around 9 p.m., the brain was relatively calm. Not thinking, but just a vague feeling that the end had arrived, created a heavy silence. The only thought was, 'I know that I am Existence. I know that I am Consciousness. Yet why am I not feeling bliss?!'

This was the moment when the thinking mind exploded with the realization that what it was trying to solve, mistaking it to be a riddle or a puzzle, was in fact a paradox! The very meaning of the word paradox is 'unsolvable'.

The intellect, having experienced first-hand that the very process of thinking requires the use of a double-hemisphere brain, that causes duality, which is the source of the paradox, suddenly broke free of the paradoxical nature of the thinking mind. As thought ended, a relaxed exhausted calmness descended. The utter indifference for and detachment from everything was far from blissful. I felt dead inside, though not despondent. Just relieved. Incapable of thinking, I lay down.

As the body relaxed, a fullness began to be felt in the chest. The emptiness that I was experiencing was filling up with something I had never known before in this being. Initially there was a racing of the heart and a shortness of breath. The whole body seemed different. There was calm and chaos simultaneously. Accompanied by a sudden and very immediate fear of death. Something gripped the heart and the thinking mind/ego came ON with the thought: is this a heart attack? But something deep within was calm and intuition was to relax and lie down. I lay down thinking if this is in fact death, it might as well be calm and meditative.

Then, the most remarkable thing happened. The heart blossomed and a strange sensation filled up and began overflowing at around 2 a.m. on 15 July. The calm ecstasy of Bliss became me.

This Bliss is Love when experienced for someone or something. When not directed outwards, it is experienced as Bliss in the heart.

8

Bliss: The Unknown, Known and the Unknowable

Bliss: This is perhaps the most misunderstood word in the entire dictionary. Bliss tends to be thought of as a pleasant or joyful or peaceful experience.

The harsh reality of Self nature is Bliss. It is absolute 'indifference' for the whole world and one realizing that though one can know that 'I am life', I cannot know what life is. Life can be explained as conscious energy, but not experienced that way. Experiencing is to know and not think.

Bliss is the relaxation the mind feels when it surrenders to the fact that life is a paradox. Paradox is an unsolvable puzzle.

For example: Which came first, the chicken or the egg?

Life is known while living and when it (I) leaves the body, that moment is called death. Apart from that, nothing can be known, by the thinking mind, as to where life goes, why it does so and what its driving force is.

The mind that surrenders to the paradox and stops its search for the meaning of life is indifferent to all aspects of living in a deep sense of detachment and relief. This experience at the end of the search for life's meaning is called Bliss.

Bliss = Back to square one but without the ego!
Bliss = Surrender to the paradox
Bliss = Detachment and indifference
Bliss = Absolute peace of mind

Experience the Unknowable

Pure Bliss = Love

'Thinking' is not 'knowing'.

'Relief,' which is initially misunderstood as 'Bliss' by the exhausted mind, upon surrender to the paradox is experienced as 'Love' in the heart on knowing that there is no paradox. It is just the limitation of a dual-natured mind, due to the dual-hemisphere human brain that sees duality where there is only one and gets frustrated at the apparent paradox.

Self nature is realized in the mind and actualized in the heart as unconditional love and service.

Life = Love

Self-Realization is experienced as Self-Actualization when the ego surrenders to the paradox of being human and God simultaneously.

9

The Whole Is Greater than the Sum of Its Parts

Any point in infinity is its centre. The heart marks that centre. The electromagnetic field around that heart centre is experienced as the personal boundary and varies in size as per the strength of the heart's vibrations. This does not refer to the physical heart that beats but the subtle vibrational field around it that causes it to beat. An individual calls this field 'my personal space'.

This electromagnetic field or aura is caused by a flow of concentrated energy in the heart centre and through the energetic pathways called nadi or meridians by the ancients. As this energy flows, a lighting up of the Consciousness in that electromagnetic field occurs, like the light surrounding a light bulb. Consciousness being the infinite and eternal field in which all of this occurs.

No matter how much science tries to prove life objectively, the simplest proof is in the subjective living experience.

Take, for example, the famous wave–particle coexistence paradox.

An intellectual mind thinks it knows the answer from quantum physics, just like a novice Zen student thinks he knows the answer to a *koan*. It is only the Zen master or a Self-Actualized One who knows that he/she is the living proof of the knowing. The experience being 'I am Consciousness, "the wave", and I am a particle, as the body in which I know that I am the wave.'

In this context, Einstein's famous equation: $E=mc^2$ understood spiritually would mean: Energy is mass vibrating with Consciousness.

This is experienced as Self-Actualized being where One feels Self as Consciousness Embodied.

10

The Giant and Her Brain and Mind

'Earth is not a platform for human life. It's a living being. We're not on it but part of it.'

—*Thomas Moore*

The giant referred to here is the One whole living organism called earth, of which the human species is the brain and the collective mind is now manifest as the Internet.

Human beings are the neurons of the world. The more we multiply, the more diverse the experience of Life for Life Itself.

It is the whole/Consciousness that makes all things occur by being whole within the seeming parts. The holographic nature of the whole is that every part reflects the whole. All separation is only an illusion created by the dualistic mind. Like One reflected by infinite mirrors. More specifically, parallel mirrors creating infinite reflections.

Every part of the whole/Consciousness acts as a partial cell of it. And the human being is the manifestation of Intelligence.

While containing all the powers of Consciousness, we exhibit the greatest one: *The Power of Will.*

Human beings are Consciousness building a giant manifestation of the collective mind via the Internet and AI.

As the human population increased on earth, the personal boundaries or energy fields began overlapping so much that it has become almost impossible to be absolutely alone in this world for even a moment. This overlapping of energy fields is like a brain full of neurons firing simultaneously.

As we know now from research done at the Heart Math Institute and the Chopra Foundation, neurons are situated not only in the brain but also the heart and Auerbach plexus and pretty much everywhere.

When each neuron/human feels itself to be separate, it is self-like, in other words: Self-ish.

When the neuron/human realizes the brain is nothing but neurons, it realizes Self. These Self-Realized neurons/humans then go around passing on the message throughout the brain until every single neuron/human knows what we are.

An amalgamation happens in the mind as the brain (humanity) feels and behaves as one due to seeing the larger picture. This feeling of Oneness is Love: The only will of Consciousness.

As we lose all privacy and become one through the Internet, Consciousness is causing the Common Collective Mind to evolve into a unified whole.

Gradually, the brain structure will evolve into a unified whole brain capable of grasping singularity instead of the duality experienced by a two-hemisphere brain. Life is constantly evolving in its physical manifestation.

What this live organism called earth does next, with human beings and computers as her brain and the Internet as her mind, is our privilege to be Conscious of!

Bonus

Always Remember:

What I am is *Life*.

Who I am is based on the *choices* I make.

Where I am is in this *body* at this *present* moment. When I am is the *Eternal* now.

Why I am is clear to me through the strongest *desires* that fill my mind and heart.

As a gift, I'm sharing with you this buffet spread of life-change methods that helped me.

Body

1. Sleep is the first medicine. It regulates neurochemicals naturally.
2. Hydrate the body. The brain is 85 per cent water.
3. A diet rich in neuron-healthy foods: green leafy vegetables, berries, nuts, omega 3- and omega 6-rich

oils, chia seeds, coconut oil, turmeric . . . Focus on eating a balanced diet of carbs, proteins and fats.

4. Exercise daily, whether it is a ten-minute brisk walk or four minutes of Tabata or longer exercise routines.

5. Breathwork: The classic pranayama is the ground of most breathwork. However, various new styles and guided sessions are available online. Find one that suits you.

6. For immediate relief try box breathing, inhale-hold-exhale-hold-inhale-hold-exhale-hold-inhale-hold-exhale. Do this till the anxiety subsides. Do breathwork daily.

7. Exposure to sunlight in the morning or evening is essential.

8. Do complete body composition tests and prioritize health and vitality.

9. Check spinal alignment and correct any imbalance.

Table of Spinal Discs and Issues Caused by Their Misalignment

Area	Chakras	Possible Inner Problems
C1	Crown	Lacking overall view, problems with the creator, desire to comprehend everything with one's head
C2	Third Eye	Lacking farsightedness, does not want to see
C3	Third Eye	Connected with the next row below
C4	Third Eye	Does not want to listen, no firm point of view, wavering loss of stability, feelings of guilt
C5	Throat	Connected with the next row below
C6	Throat	Inability to speak well, unable to bite one's way through the lump in the throat
C7	Throat	Feels humiliated, suppressed, suffers silence, no defence
T1	Throat	Happily overburdens oneself, shoulders carry a great deal, does everything by oneself, no trust
T2	Heart	Finds it difficult to be loving, locks one's heart, joyless
T3	Heart	Wants nothing for oneself, puts oneself last, does not want to breathe deeply, no own opinion
T4	Heart	Inner anger, lets nothing out, single-minded, embittered
T5	Solar plexus	Worries over others, problems with the 'inner child', neglects own vital interests, always sad, cries a lot
T6	Solar plexus	Connected with the next row below
T7	Solar plexus	Swallows a great deal, lets nothing out, loses oneself in addictions to eating, drinking, etc., internal rebelling

Area	Chakras	Possible Inner Problems
T8	Solar plexus	Worries rigid, does not surrender to the flow of life
T9	Solar plexus	Suppresses own aggression, makes accusations, allergic
T10	Solar plexus	Partnership problems with parents or husband, wife, children, colleagues, neighbours and other people
T11	Solar plexus	Contact problems, insecurity, fear, feels weak, afraid
T12	Solar plexus	Connected with the next row below
L1	Solar plexus	Finds it hard to make a new start, fearful and can't let go of things in the past, e.g. parents, partners, people, animals, places of residence, property, work, career, etc.
L2	Solar plexus	Becomes defensive very quickly, feelings of panic
L3	Sacral	Connected with the next row below
L4	Sacral	Connected with the next row below
L5	Sacral	Sexual problems, lethargy in 'digesting' problems, lack of security, feelings of guilt
Sacral	Sacral	How do I carry the burden of life?
Coccyx	Root	Lacking a connection to Mother Earth

Area	Organ Connection	Possible Physical Problems
C1	Head, optical nerve, brain	Headaches, migraines, high blood pressure, chronic tiredness, dizziness, paralysis due to irregular circulation in brain
C2	Eyes, tongue, ears, sinuses	Sinus problems, eye trouble, deafness, ear pains
C3	Ears, teeth, facial nerves	Pain in face nerves, spots, acne, tinnitus, toothache, bad teeth, plaque, bleeding gums, neuralgia
C4	Nose, mouth, lips, ears, mandibular joint, throat	Constant cold, loss of hearing, chapped lips, cramped lip muscles, adenoids, catarrh
C5	Cervical muscles, throat, neck	Hoarseness, sore throat, chronic cold, laryngitis
C6	Acromioclavicular joint, shoulder, tonsils, neck	Tonsillitis, croup, stiff neck, upper arm pains, whooping cough and goitre
C7	Thyroid gland, elbow, sternoclavicular joint	Diseases of the thyroid gland, cuts, bursitis in the shoulder or elbow, depression, fear
T1	Shoulder, wrist, hand, neck, lower arm, fingers	Shoulder pains, neck cramps, lower arm/hand pains, ligament inflammations, furry feeling in fingers
T2	Heart, blood vessels, chest	Heart trouble, disruption in rhythm, fears, chest pains
T3	Lungs, skin, breasts, chest, mammary gland	Bronchitis, influenza, pleurisy, pneumonia, cough, breathing difficulties, asthma, disruption in chest region
T4	Gall bladder, tendons, ligaments	Trouble in the gall bladder, gall stones, jaundice, headaches on one side (from gall bladder meridian)

Area	Organ Connection	Possible Physical Problems
T5	Liver, circulatory system, immune system, tendons, ligaments	Disruptions in liver, low blood pressure, anaemia, fatigue, shingles, circulatory weakness, arthritis
T6	Stomach, muscles, pancreas	Stomach and digestion problems, heartburn, diabetes
T7	Duodenum, stomach, pancreas, muscles	Duodenal ulcers, stomach complaints, hiccups, possible lack of vitamins, weakness
T8	Spleen, blood, muscles	Spleen problems, weakness in the immune system
T9	Adrenal gland	Allergies, nettle rash
T10	Kidney, bones	Kidney problems, salt cannot get out, chalked-up arteries, chronic tiredness
T11	Skin, kidney, urinary track, bones	Skin diseases, acne, spots, eczema, boils, raw skin psoriasis (does not drink enough, needs more liquid)
T12	Small intestine, ovary, testicles, blood vessels, circulation	Problems with the small intestine, wind, rheumatism, disruption in growth, infertility, erectile dysfunction
L1	Large intestine, skin	Problems with large intestine, disruption in circulation, intestine blockages, diarrhoea, constipation
L2	Large bowel, appendix, skin	Problems with appendix, stomach cramps, hyperacidity, varicose veins
L3	Bladder, uterus, prostate, knee	Problems during pregnancy, menstrual pain, menopause problems, bladder pain, knee aches, often together with the bladder, impotence, bed-wetting
L4	Sigmoid, sciatic nerve, prostate	Sciatica, lumbago, prostate trouble, painful or too frequent urination (daily massage of buttock muscles)

Area	Organ Connection	Possible Physical Problems
L5	Rectum	Circulation problems in legs and feet, cold feet, cramps in caves, swelling of feet and legs
Sacral	Sacrum, legs, hip, sciatic nerve, crest, buttocks, genital organs	Sciatica, abdominal problems, chronic constipation, pains in legs and feet
Coccyx	Anus	Haemorrhoids, itching anus pain on sitting

Mind

1. The biggest obstacle to any change is the existing conditioning/programme in our subconscious mind. This automatic set of paradigms and points of view are deeply grooved in the brain and were created by a lifetime of repetition and reinforcement. The easiest way to rewrite the subconscious programmes is hypnosis. Find a good hypnotherapist or listen to specific deep hypnosis programmes that will heal deep-seated issues. I personally used Marisa Peer's RTT (Rapid Transformational Hypnotherapy). Preferably use these hypnotic tracks every night for 21–41 days to rewire your brain out of its old patterns.

2. Learn about the mind, its workings, psychology, the brain, neurophysiology, and neurochemistry as much as possible.

3. Take time to do standardized personality tests.

4. Keep a journal, physical or digital. Journaling organizes the mind and clears up the path for fresh ideas and intuition.

5. Make a list of your passions and work on them every day. Check how you can be of service.

6. Tackle anxiety with a clear goal of addressing the pressing problem. Answer all areas of an issue that worries you, then decide to take it as it comes for things that are not in your control.

7. Systematically study your core beliefs about every area in life and discard old outdated beliefs. Keep only beliefs that empower.

8. Do not accept or agree with any labels that are given to you. Everything changes.

9. Make lists of all desires and ideas.

10. Learn to access and trust your intuition.

Energy

1. Be very specific about the vibes of the people you are around. Stay away from those who blame, shame, criticize or complain. The victim mentality is highly contagious.

2. Travel or spend time in natural settings—mountains, beaches, forests, rain, wind and sunlight.

3. Walk barefoot in the grass or in mud if possible. It is grounding and stabilizing. It connects your root chakra to the ground and allows an easier flow of energy.

4. Laugh. Watch funny videos or stand-up comedy and comedy movies. Or just laugh, as in a laughter club.

5. Learn energy work—chakra systems and several others. Balancing energies and being aware of one's energy bodies is key to deep healing. If you are new to the realm of energy, these simple techniques will blow your mind. Some methods that helped me came from Eden Energy Medicine, Chakra healing sessions, classic yoga and qigong.

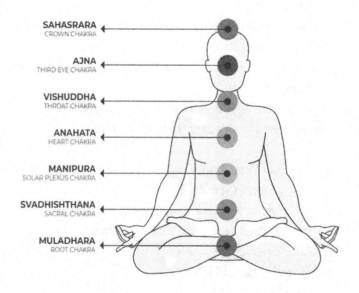

SAHASRARA
CROWN CHAKRA

AJNA
THIRD EYE CHAKRA

VISHUDDHA
THROAT CHAKRA

ANAHATA
HEART CHAKRA

MANIPURA
SOLAR PLEXUS CHAKRA

SVADHISHTHANA
SACRAL CHAKRA

MULADHARA
ROOT CHAKRA

To Enhance Consciousness

1. Meditate.
2. Constantly be mindful of whether you are fully present in the body.
3. Read, learn and listen to consciousness-expanding material.

4. Be humble, honest and receptive when you ask for help.

5. Learn about something from the vast unknown every day.

6. Design a healthy morning routine that will make the start of the day effective and automatic. Fill it with healthy practices for body, mind, energy and consciousness.

7. Design a healthy night routine that helps you unwind and rejuvenate.

8. Spend relaxing time doing nothing for at least ten minutes every day.

9. If you are struggling with existential angst, try some of the greatest classics ever. They helped me.

    a. *Tao Te Ching*, Lao Tzu
    b. Ashtavakra Geetha
    c. *Devi Kalothara*, Ramana Maharshi
    d. *Vivekachudamani*, Adi Shankaracharya
    e. The Upanishads
    f. The Bhagavad Gita
    g. The Uddhava Gita

10. Listening to relaxing music, especially classical music, has deep soothing and healing effects.

11. Access Consciousness Bars sessions and Jose Silva's methods are great tools.

12. Learn the healing and transformation capabilities of crystals and essential oils.

13. Most importantly, be patient and kind with yourself and the world.

Table of Dimensions

D	Realm	Cause	Effect	Remedy
1D	Physical	Cellular memory	Sense of individual ego	1. Spiritual wisdom 2. Humanity practices 3. Panchakarma to remove Vasanas (tendencies) by genetic (mutation) rewriting 4. Solitude, especially away from family
2D	Ethereal	Energy fields Chakras Prana Aura Life energy	Personal space	Pranic healing Yogasanas Pranayam Chakra healing Qigong, reiki
3D	Astral	Planets and stars Universe	Collective mind Collective energy field Gravitational	Vedic astrology Einstein's and other metaphysical studies, quantum physics
4D	Mind	Collective mind working as ancestry/ conditioning tradition, etc. (100th monkey)	Individuality, feeling of isolation, existential angst, depression, anxiety, stress	1. Study of the mind through scriptural education 2. Contemplation 3. Meditation

D	Realm	Cause	Effect	Remedy
5D. a)	Spiritual	Spiritual ignorance	Delusion (Avidya Maya) Ego–World–Mind	Mind has to end in meditation through devotion/ faith/scriptures, contemplation, prayer/intention
b)		Spiritual wisdom	End of delusion Self-Realization	
6D	Cosmic	Self-Realization	Self-Actualization	Meditation Silence
7D	Transcendence (Samadhi)	Self-Actualization (Jeevan Mukthi)	Embodied consciousness/ Bliss/Love	(Videha Mukthi) Liberation from body at death

Map of Consciousness
Developed by David R. Hawkins

The Map of Consciousness is based on a logarithmic
scale that spans from 0 to 1000.

Name of Level	Energetic "Frequency"	Associated Emotional State	View of Life
Enlightenment	700–1000	Ineffable	Is
Peace	600	Bliss	Perfect
Joy	540	Serenity	Complete
Love	500	Reverence	Benign
Reason	400	Understanding	Meaningful
Acceptance	350	Forgiveness	Harmonious
Willingness	310	Optimism	Hopeful
Neutrality	250	Trust	Satisfactory
Courage	200	Affirmation	Feasible
Pride	175	Scorn	Demanding
Anger	150	Hate	Antagonistic
Desire	125	Craving	Disappointing
Fear	100	Anxiety	Frightening
Grief	75	Regret	Tragic
Apathy	50	Despair	Hopeless
Guilt	30	Blame	Evil
Shame	20	Humiliation	Miserable

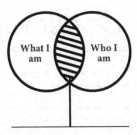

Personality (how I show up) in the world

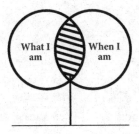

Consciousness (level of awareness)

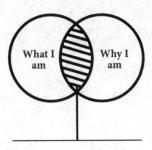

Purpose (doing what I love and bringing it to its highest potential and a contribution to life and the world)

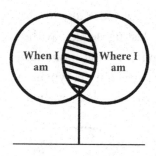

Presence (Being Here–Now/Now–Here)

1. Here–Now is being fully present in the physical body. It is ideal for showing up fully in the world. (Outward-directed presence.)
2. Being Now–Here fully present as the energy vibration that one is—in essence and uniqueness, is the best pathway for meditation, intuition and creativity. (The word itself looks like 'I am nowhere'.) Being nowhere is to be everywhere. (Inward-directed presence.)

Either way, conscious awareness of when and where I am makes for spectacular experiences in/of/as life.

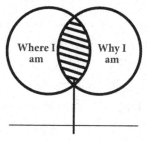

Contribution (the legacy I leave behind)

Conscious, present, purposeful and service-oriented living leaves behind a lasting legacy without it having been thoughtfully planned by the individual. The grand design of the universe is perfect in the synchronized working of its parts because the universe is one whole organism.

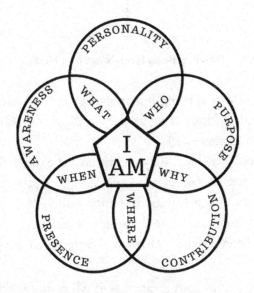

The Whole = Every Thing & No Thing

This all-inclusiveness of every stage of consciousness is what makes us strive for Self-Actualization. Actualization feels like irresponsibility to the mind.

To actualize is to live out one's full potential. Only you will know the feeling of fulfilment of actualization but in getting there you would have made everything on the way better for everyone. They may realize it much later.

Internal and external regulation become autonomic. Like all the mind's work is taken over by consciousness. Just as the autonomic nervous system keeps the internal organs perfectly functional without the mind's control, such as for breathing and heart function, similarly, for an actualized being, all the previously cognitive functions go on auto-pilot. The thinking mind was in fact the cause of all suffering. Life just lives itself!

'In the end, it all makes sense. If it doesn't make sense, it is not the end.'

Epilogue

In 2017, when I quit taking psychiatric medication on my own responsibility and trusted the clinical psychologist I am, I knew it wouldn't be easy. But I also knew that it was my responsibility. I promised myself that if I would come out of the last episode that withdrawal from the medication would cause, and stay stable and evolve for two years, I would write a book about all the alternative methods that helped me and my realizations along the way. My hope is that it may contribute to others on this path and save them the troubles I went through in some small way. Here I am, five years later, at the best I've ever been in my life. As I celebrate the silver jubilee of my acting career, it seemed befitting to share the story behind the scenes.

Immortality

One who has realized the true nature of Self/I as Life/Consciousness/God/Love has only one purpose in living. To be of service to the world.

It is in loving, selfless service that immortality is. This person is remembered every day in the hearts of all that were touched and continues to make the world a better place through those who remember. Thus, continuing the ancestry of spiritual transformation.

Life/Love is immortal. May you experience yourself as that.

Self-realization is nothing more than the 'Aha!' moments that happen in the mind as one realizes what One-Self is. If you have had those experiences while reading this book, CONGRATULATIONS! Click on the QR code below to download the certificate of Self-Realization, to be authorized by the only One who knows the truth by experience— the One you call 'I'.

Disclaimer

Do not stop taking any medication without consulting your doctor.
Wishing you conscious living and the eternal bliss that comes from knowing and experiencing.

Love, Lenaa

Scan QR code to access the
Penguin Random House India website